ROMANTICISM AND THE GOTHIC REVIVAL

SWEDENBORGIAN CATHEDRAL AT BRYN ATHYN, PENNSYLVANIA, 1913-28
RALPH ADAMS CRAM, ARCHITECT

ROMANTICISM
AND THE
GOTHIC REVIVAL

BY

AGNES ADDISON, Ph.D.

INSTRUCTOR IN HISTORY OF ART
UNIVERSITY OF PENNSYLVANIA

1967
GORDIAN PRESS, INC
NEW YORK

018459

Copyright, 1938, by RICHARD R. SMITH,
120 East 39th Street, New York, N. Y.

———

All rights reserved. No part of this book may be reproduced
in any form without permission of the publisher.

Reprinted by GORDIAN PRESS, INC. with permission
of RICHARD R. SMITH CO., INC. 1967
Library of Congress Catalog Card Number 67-18439

Printed in U.S.A. by
EDWARDS BROTHERS, INC.
Ann Arbor, Michigan

TO
MY PARENTS

FOREWORD

SINCE THE Middle Ages and the fall of United Christendom, three distinct architectural styles have appeared, each of which expresses the fundamental ideals and aspirations of their time. The first two consciously derive their inspiration from a past style. The third, the contemporary International Style, differs from its predecessors in that it tries to break away from all historical styles and to use only the materials and the necessities of the present as a basis for artistic expression. The first of the modern styles, the Renaissance, turned to the ruins of Rome to evolve its architectural idiom, for the men of the Renaissance felt a kinship with the classical period of antiquity and only scorn and contempt for the "old-fashioned" and "barbaric" art and ideals of their mediaeval forefathers. The intermediate style which bridged the years between the Renaissance and the contemporary period is the subject of the present work. It is the style of Romanticism and the Gothic Revival which broke with the classic tradition as interpreted by the Renaissance and turned to the Middle Ages for spiritual and artistic inspiration.

To Dr. William Lingelbach, Professor of Modern European History in the University of Pennsylvania, I am indebted for suggesting the subject and for encouragement and criticism. I wish to acknowledge the kindness of Dr. Leicester B. Holland, Chief of the Division of Fine Arts of the Library of Congress and Professor of Fine Arts in

vii

the University of Pennsylvania, of Dr. Conyers Read, Professor of English History in the University of Pennsylvania, and of Dr. Fiske Kimball, Director of the Philadelphia Museum of Art, for critically reading the manuscript and making helpful suggestions. To the many people who have welcomed me to their churches, monasteries, houses and civic buildings as I have pursued my study of the Gothic Revival in England, France, Canada and the United States, I am happy to here express my appreciation of their friendly assistance. In the course of the work I have read in libraries in London, Paris, Toronto, Boston, Cambridge, New York, Washington, Chicago and Philadelphia, and have everywhere met with unfailing courtesy and helpfulness.

A. A.

Philadelphia, 1938.

CONTENTS

018459

ROMANTICISM AND THE
GOTHIC REVIVAL

CHAPTER I

ROMANTICISM AND THE ROMANTIC PERIOD

THE WORD romanticism, according to the Oxford Shorter Dictionary, was first used in 1803. It was used to describe the contemporary literary movement which found inspiration in mediaeval romances and in personal experiences, especially those of the imagination, and expressed itself in free forms which were not derived from classic canons.

Romanticism in most phases was anti-classical, so it is interesting to note that the word ultimately derived from Roma, the name of the capital of the greatest classical empire. With the spread of the Roman empire went the language of Rome. Even after the Empire of Rome disintegrated and the barbarian kingdoms succeeded, the language remained in a changed and debased form in the Italic and Iberian peninsulas, in Gaul and about the lower Danube. By the eighth century this debased Latin went by the name, *lingua Romanica*. By the fourteenth century, after a thousand years of evolution five principal languages emerged from the *lingua Romanica:* Spanish, Italian, French, Portuguese and Rumanian. These then were called Romance languages and the metrical narratives composed in these dialects, romans.

In the fourteenth and fifteenth centuries these romans were introduced into English literature through the works of Chaucer, Caxton and Malory. Since these Romances had originally been recited, they had a free form which they retained even after they were written down. These Romances were tales of adventure, chivalry and ideal love. So when the word Romance and the many words derived from it were first used in the English language in the seventeenth century, the meaning was directly derived from the contemporary opinion of the mediaeval romans, that is fictitious or a lying tale, strange or fantastic. The adjective romantic, from which the noun romanticism was directly derived, had many shades of meaning added to it from its first usage in 1659 as fictitious until 1803. It was very often used to describe scenery which affected the emotions. John Evelyn wrote, "There is also, on the side of this horrid alp, a very romantic seat." [1] Addison also used it in 1701. "It is so Romantic a scene, that it has always probably given occasion to such Chimerical Relations." [2]

Two quotations from Mrs. Radcliffe's novels written at the end of the eighteenth century just before the word romanticism was coined give a clear notion of the use of the adjective. "On the northeast coast of Scotland, in the most romantic part of the Highlands, stood the castle of Athlin: an edifice built on a summit of a rock whose base was in the sea. This pile was venerable from its antiquity, and from its Gothic structure; but more venerable from the virtues which it enclosed." [3] "He approached, and perceived the Gothic remains of an abbey; it stood on a kind of rude lawn, overshadowed by high and spreading trees, which seemed coeval with the building and diffused a romantic gloom around." [4] Romantic was a synonym for strange,

---

[1] *Diary*, June 27, 1654.   [2] *Letters from Italy*, I, 359.
[3] *Castle of Athlin and Dunboyne*, 1789.
[4] *Romance of the Forest*, 1791.

remote, ancient, fantastic, awe-inspiring, melancholic, sentimental. Toward the end of the century it was used also interchangeably with Gothic which was used in architecture to describe anything which was not classical. Hurd [5] uses Gothic to describe non-classical literature and it is from this relation to Gothic that romantic derived its nineteenth century meaning of the antithesis to classic, which it originally did not have.

More and more writers by 1800 were using romantic subjects, describing romantic situations or romantic sentiments, so naturally the word romanticism was introduced to name this literature and the writers were called Romanticists.

It was not until 1840 and after, that in England critics began trying to analyze the Romantic Movement, to differentiate its main characteristics. The first creative period was over by then. These general characteristics were a reaction against classic canons; an emphasis on the individual; reliance on the imagination rather than on the reason; a new interest in the Middle Ages and a revival of Christianity; a pride in national history and a curiosity about the culture and literature of other countries. In expression these tendencies focussed in a revival of lyric poetry. Change, variety and emotion were highly prized by the Romantics and were the keynotes of the Romantic Movement.

The Romantic period in history might be arbitrarily dated from 1775 to 1840. In political history it is the Age of Revolutions which comes between the Ancien Régime of the Monarchies and the succeeding period of Imperialism. In economic history, it is the period of *laissez-faire*. In

[5] *Letters on Chivalry and Romance,* 1762.

political theory, it is the Age of Democracy. In literature, it is the time of the Romantic Schools. In architecture, it is the period of the Greek and Gothic revivals.

In the last hundred years many books have been written stressing one or the other of these characteristics and finding others. F. L. Lucas [6] says that he has gnawed his way through 11,396 books on the subject and there may be more. Two definite changes in the term romanticism have come out of all this writing. One is that the term is no longer restricted to literature but is considered as a *Zeitgeist* of the early nineteenth century. The other is that romanticism or the romantic spirit is no longer considered the exclusive property of the Romantic Movement, but is found to be a fundamental and ever recurring phenomenon of artistic creation.

Three definitions of this eternal romanticism follow. The author of each is an Englishman writing in this century. The first of the three, chronologically, is that given by Geoffrey Scott, a fervent admirer of the Renaissance. "Romanticism may be said to consist in a high development of poetic sensibility towards the remote, as such. It idealises the distant, both of time and place." [7] According to this, all revivals are romantic in origin, the Renaissance as well as the Gothic Revival.

The other two writers are literary critics. Lascelles Abercrombie wrote in 1927: [8] ". . . we may say that it [romanticism] is clearly *a tendency away from actuality*. We see the spirit of the mind withdrawing more and more from commerce with the outer world, and endeavouring, or at

[6] *Decline and Fall of the Romantic Ideal,* p. 3.
[7] *Architecture of Humanism,* p. 39.
[8] *Romanticism,* p. 49.

least desiring, to rely more and more on the things it finds within itself." "It is when inner experience assumes the first importance, still more when it assumes the only importance, in the composite fact of life, that romanticism appears. Indeed, for a general proposition, romanticism can hardly be defined more precisely than a *tendency* to rely on the inner experience." [9] F. L. Lucas [10] writing in 1936 has been influenced by Freud's analysis of the ego. "If I had to hazard an Aristotelian definition of Romanticism, it might run—'Romantic literature is a dream-picture of life; providing sustenance and fulfilment for impulses cramped by society or reality.'"

Romanticism is the love of change for its own sake. The romantic spirit is never satisfied with what it has. It either wants what went before, as Pugin wished to recreate the Middle Ages, or it wants what someone else has, as the Pre-Romantics in France wished for English constitutionalism. Naturally, romantic literature is emotional and imaginative, for the emotions are notoriously mercurial and the imagination is free from the fetters of time and space and the curbs of plausibility and possibility. This definition is applicable to all periods of romantic creation and well describes the fundamental characteristic of the Romantic period.

Nevertheless, before considering more fully nineteenth-century romanticism, it seems necessary to say a word about another aspect of this subject which so interests critics, and that is its relation to classicism. They are generally considered to be antithetical. Reason *versus* Emotion. Scott, who is writing of architecture, considers classicism the architecture of humanism. "To pass from Roman

[9] *Ibid.*, p. 125.   [10] *Op. cit.*, pp. 35–6.

architecture and that of the Renaissance to the fantastic
and bewildered energy of Gothic, is to leave humanism for
magic, the study of the congruous for the cult of the
strange." [11] He feels that the humanistic values of classicism are at variance with the uncontrolled expression of the
romantic.

Abercrombie sees in realism the antithesis of romanticism and in classicism the perfect equilibrium of all elements.[12] Lucas has a different idea. "Classicism, Romanticism, Realism are three extremes, three points of a
triangle; the magic circle lies inscribed within it." [13]

Classicism might be defined as the love of continuous
growth. There is change in growth, but it is gradual and so,
almost imperceptible. The difficulty in using these words
arises from the obvious fact that no abstract terms can ade-
quately describe the manifold expression of human history.
Not everyone wanted change in the Romantic period; the
French nobility did not. Another confusion arises because
the Romantics were not rebelling against the classic principle, but against the classicistic which stultifies growth by
setting rigid standards and admitting no variations. It was
the Three Unities of Corneille, not of Aristotle, against
which Victor Hugo revolted.

Whatever may be the exact relationship of the romanticism of 1800 to the classicism of 1700, they are not the
same at all events. The difficulty is to say when the difference first appeared: to pin it down and say here was planted
the first seed of romanticism.

Everyone knows that there was a Romantic Movement
in European literature in the early nineteenth century and

[11] Scott, *op. cit.*, p. 24.   [13] Lucas, *op. cit.*, p. 139.
[12] Abercrombie, *op. cit.*, p. 33.

that Scott, Byron, Shelley, Hugo, Lamartine, de Vigny, Heine, Novalis, Mazzoni, and Espronceda were representatives of this school. We know that the first symptoms of the Movement are to be found in the eighteenth century in a growth of sentiment and pleasing melancholy, in a boredom with the classical forms of art, in a new interest in Nature, in landscape, the simple life, the Noble Savage and the Chinese Sage. There was a general malaise which culminated in nineteenth-century romanticism, which Goethe defined as disease.

But where did this disease start, or was it like a plague brought with the wind? J. Robertson [14] would suggest that it was a south wind, for he sees *The Genesis of Romantic Theory* in the Italian Society of the Arcadians founded in 1694 and to be discerned in the writings of Gravina, Muratori, Vico and Martelli. They are the forerunners of the social and political ideas rather than exponents of romantic literature.

M. Seillière [15] is quite sure that it is a disease, the *mal romantique,* and has written many books to prove its source in J. J. Rousseau. Jacques Maritain in *Three Reformers* has tried to whitewash him to a certain extent, for Rousseau was a Roman Catholic. Yet he says, "We all know what romanticism got from him." [16] In a footnote he amplifies this statement by defining romanticism. "In so far as it signifies a religious eviction of reason and its works, the sacred unbridling of sensation, the holy parade of self, and the adoration of primitive natural instinct, pantheism as theology, and emotional stimulus as the rule of life, it must be confessed that Rousseau, by his mystical natural-

[14] *The Genesis of Romantic Theory.*
[15] *Romantisme.*   [16] *Three Reformers,* p. 115.

ism, is at the direct source of such a spiritual evil." By the French, Rousseau is generally considered the forerunner of romanticism. It is true that he emphasized self, emotions and change, but he was more of a reformer than a true Romantic. He absorbed the ideas of Locke on the importance of education, and the ideas of Hobbes on the origin of government in the social contract theory.[17] He transformed these notions to produce his own creed of the natural goodness of man and the corruptness of contemporary civilization. His works were much read, and he himself was greatly admired in the eighteenth century. He certainly did a great deal to arouse the sensibilities of the French and so prepare for the Romantic Movement, and his influence was not confined to his own country, but was great in Germany and the American colonies.

Some see the first glimmer of romanticism in the poetry of Klopstock and Haller and the Swiss Nature poets. Others turn to the English Nature poets of the 1740's. A few writers see a continuous expression of romanticism in English literature, for one, Harko de Maar, in his *History of Modern English Romanticism.* All that seems certain is that by 1750 the first break with the Classicists had become evident in France, Germany and England.

It is a fascinating subject to study, for there were so many similarities in the expression of the Romantic Movement, and yet differences. The influences of one country upon another is also a knotty problem. In Spain and Italy the movement seems definitely to have been imported. It was not indigenous in France either; the early romanticism

---

[17] Jules Vuÿ, *Origines des Idées politique de Rousseau,* suggests the charter of Geneva given May 23, 1387, by the prince-bishop, Adémar Fabri as the source for Rousseau's theory.

came from England and the later from Germany. There was an interchange of ideas between England and Germany. Sturm und Drang poetry and drama was translated into English in the last decade of the eighteenth century. Shakespeare was one of the great literary heroes of the German Romanticists. Both countries were early ready to receive romanticism, for the Classicists were never so firmly intrenched as they had been in France. One thing is certain: that is, that the peak of the Romantic Movement in Germany came earlier than in other countries.

The date often arbitrarily given for the beginning of the Movement in Germany is 1773, the date of the publication of *Von Deutscher Art und Kunst,* a collection of essays by Herder, Möser and Goethe. The dominating interests of the movement were first expressed here: the Middle Ages, free lyric forms, nationalism, and Gothic art, and the appreciation of Shakespeare. German literature developed very fast in the sixty years until 1833 when Heine wrote *Die Romantische Schule,* for in those years is the history of the Romantic Movement in Germany. The first years witnessed the apprenticeship or Sturm und Drang period of which Goethe's *Werther* is the best known example. That was the dramatic and emotional side; the other was antiquarian and historical and resulted in the collection of folk songs by Tieck and the fairy tales by the brothers Grimm. By 1798 with the formation of the Jena group the movement was reaching its peak in the writings of Hardenberg (Novalis), the Schlegels and Schleiermacher. By 1806 the young Romantics with Arnim, Brentano, Hoffmann and Heine were writing. Goethe held himself aloof from the romantic writers, but his *Goetz* and above all his *Faust* are romantic in treatment, form and subject matter. By 1812 he was quite scornful of the movement and engaged in planning the Welt Literatur and psychic research (*Elective Affinities*). Germany was more influenced by the discovery of the Middle Ages than any other country. It was reflected not only in verse forms, in subject matter of poems and plays, but also in a new national pride which Fichte did so much to foster. The Italians of the Renaissance and the French of the Classic period had been rather scornful of the boorish Germans, so naturally it pleased them to realize that their Teutonic ancestors had caused the fall of Rome, and that their primitive society had given freedom to the individual. Mediaevalism is the most important characteristic of German romanticism. The second is a philosophic approach discernible in all their writing, prose or poetry, rather than sheer lyricism or sensationalism.

Elements of romanticism are to be found in all periods of English literature. The great poets of the sixteenth century, Spenser, Sidney, Shakespeare, wrote before the lyric, imaginative style and mood of the mediaeval romans had been banished by classic canons. In England their works were always read and their influence is discernible in every period. Dryden and Milton were imaginative poets, also. *Paradise Lost*, the *Faerie Queene* and the plays of Shakespeare became the models for the romantic poets on the continent. Voltaire wrote, "It is a pity that there is more barbarism than genius in the works of Shakespeare."[18] That was the classic attitude. Herder expresses the romantic when he says, "Fortunately, I live in a time when I can understand Shakespeare."[19] Since Shakespeare was always admired in England, the admiration for the Greeks could

[18] *Essai sur les Moeurs*, III:158.
[19] "Shakespeare" in *Von deutscher Art und Kunst*, p. 208.

never be so despotic as it became in France. Yet the meta-
physical poets cannot be called Romantics, for they were
more interested in the turn of phrase and mental gymnas-
tics than in the lyric expression of the imagination, nor can
Pope with his heroic couplets, his translations and witty
Dunciad be considered a member of the Romantic School.

Sometimes, therefore, the date of the death of Alexander
Pope is given for the beginning of the Romantic Movement
in English literature. That is 1744, and at the same time
the Graveyard Poets were writing their melancholy and
morbid verses. They were swiftly followed by the more
charming and cheerful Nature Poets, but they were often
touched by gentle sadness. In Gray's *Elegy written in a
Country Churchyard* there is a line in the Epitaph:

"And Melancholy mark'd him for her own."

which well describes the author.

In the sixties came the renewed interest in ballads and
the original ones of Thomas Chatterton. One of the best of
his ballads, from the *Song from Ælla*, has the following
refrain:

"My love is dead,
Gone to his death-bed
All under the willow tree."

The literati of the end of the century had their taste
whetted by the "Tales of Horror" in which the supernatural
and the fantastic played important roles.

All through the century there was a current of romantic
literature, yet it was not the dominant force until after
1798. In that year was published the *Lyrical Ballads*, a
collection of poems by Coleridge and by Wordsworth, which

included *The Rime of the Ancient Mariner* and *Tintern Abbey*. These two poems typify as well as any the main characteristics of the Romantic Movement in England. Both are truly poetic in expression, and the words are so exquisitely chosen that they enhance the meaning without intruding themselves upon the reader. Coleridge's poem gives the most intense reality to the unreal, the supernatural and the fantastic.

> "The very deep did rot: O Christ!
> That ever this should be!
> Yea, slimy things did crawl with legs
> Upon the slimy sea."

It arouses a strong emotional reaction in the reader, and was written with startling imagery.

A completely different aspect of the Movement is expressed by Wordsworth in *Tintern*. It is equally emotional, but calmer, more mystic. The main themes of the poem are the eternal beauty of nature, the power of nature to console the human spirit and the source of this beauty in the spirit of God.

> "I have felt
> A presence that disturbs me with the joy
> Of elevated thoughts; a sense sublime
> Of something far more deeply interfused,
> Whose dwelling is the light of setting suns,
> And the round ocean, and the living air,
> And the blue sky, and in the mind of man;"

The peak of the Romantic Movement in English literature was about 1815. The lyric quality of the poetry and the beauty of wording binds together the romantic poets more than subject matter. Nature, Greece, love and the Middle Ages were the main sources of inspiration. By 1824 and the death of Byron the first phase of the Movement was almost over. Keats and Shelley were dead. Wordsworth had finished writing great poetry. Scott had become a novelist, the greatest of all romantic novelists, but his lyric days were over. Romanticism was healthiest in England, not so intense, frenetic, and its best quality was lyricism.

Even though the Romantic Movement may be considered to be over in the first quarter of the century, the prevalence of romanticism in English literature of the rest of the century and in contemporary writing is recognized. In the novels of Dickens there are many romantic touches. The Pre-Raphaelite Brotherhood of the 1850's is often considered a part of the Romantic Movement. Tennyson and the Brownings have many characteristics of a Romantic. Even the neo-classicism of Arnold has romantic tendencies. In the present century de la Mare, Noyes and A. E. Housman have written romantic poetry. In English literature the romantic element is almost always present in some degree.

In France it is otherwise. There was an important and striking Romantic Movement, but the fundamental attitude of the French mind is reasonable rather than imaginative. All through the eighteenth century there were symptoms of romanticism. Paul Hazard considers Abbé Prevost a pre-romantique, because of his novel *Manon Lescaut* published in 1731. Abbé de Saint-Pierre is another with his schemes for improving almost everything, even the world, by *Perpetual Peace*. By 1760 the Abbé Galiani could shock Diderot by confessing that he had never shed a tear in his life.[20] Before the Revolution the cultivated French-

[20] Becker, *Heavenly City*, p. 41.

man had become very sentimental as can be seen in the paintings of Greuze and Chardin. The name generally given to this sensibility is Rococo, which is very similar to romanticism but has the fundamental difference of being avowedly artificial.

In 1789, the Revolution came and men's minds were sharply focussed on contemporary events and politics. Most of the writing was for pamphlets or journals. The one great poet of the period, André Chénier, was guillotined and his poetry is admired especially for its classical purity of expression.

"Sur des pensers nouveaux faisons des vers antiques." [21]

It was not until after the Goddess of Reason had been worshipped in Notre-Dame and found wanting that the romantic spirit triumphed. The first step was the publication of *Le Génie du Christianisme* by Chateaubriand in 1802. This turned men's minds back to the Christian Church, to the Middle Ages and to the mystery of the infinite. His works, *René, Atala, Memoires,* all betray the romantic temperament. The second step was Madame de Staël's *De l'Allemagne,* by which Schlegel's idea of the romanticism of northern peoples as opposed to the classicism of the southern countries was made known in France, in 1813.[22] Another important book which may be said to usher in the Romantic Movement in France was the novel *Adolphe,* written by Benjamin Constant in 1814.[23] It gives the keynote of introspection, hysteria and morbid imaginings which characterize so much of the period.

[21] Chénier, *L'Invention,* l. 184.
[22] First edition of 1810 was confiscated; second ed. 1813.
[23] Published in 1816.

The Romantic Movement really began in France with the Restoration. There was a natural reaction against the formal classicism of the court of Napoleon. This was aided by the return of émigrés from England and Switzerland, who had been influenced during their travels by the Romantic Movements in Germany and England. All classes of society found something pleasing in romanticism and so the vogue grew quickly and intensely. The classic tradition was so much stronger in France than elsewhere that the reaction was much stronger. The new freedom of expression and emotionalism went to their heads like an intoxicant and there was a veritable delirium during the decade 1825–35. In the midst of this period came the July Revolution which turned their thoughts again to politics and to liberalism. Hugo defined romanticism as liberalism in literature.[24] The peak of the Romantic Movement in France was 1830. In February *Hernani* by Victor Hugo was presented and precipitated the struggle between the Classicists and the Romantics, in which the latter were successful, and in July came the Revolution which resulted in the Bourgeois King and Romanticists in government positions.

The Romantic Movement in France was short-lived but intense. The Romantics triumphed in 1830 and so soon they became conservative and the Realists shocked in their turn. As early as 1836 Alfred de Musset in the first of the *Lettres de Dupuis et Cotonet* made fun of the vagaries of romanticism although he was one of *les vrais romantiques de 1830*. By 1843 *Les Burgraves* of Victor Hugo bored the public. In the same year Louis Reybaud wrote a most penetrating satire on the foibles and extravagances of the

[24] Preface to *Hernani*, 1830.

short-lived, but intense period of romanticism in his book, *Jérôme Paturot à la recherche d'une position sociale*. The public became weary even of the adventurous tales of Dumas père, and turned with relief to the novels of Balzac and later to those of Zola and the social comedies of Dumas, fils.

Perhaps it is too arbitrary to say that soon after 1840, when the Romantic Movement was over, all romanticism died out of French literature. But at least it changed and did not become evident until after 1870 with the Symbolist poets and Baudelaire and Verlaine, and recently in a psychopathic form in the writings of Apollinaire and the Surrealists.

The two main characteristics of the French Romantic Movement which differentiate it from the others were a strong reaction against classicism as embodied in *l'art classique* of Louis XIV and a close alliance with politics.

In the literature of the United States there is nothing comparable to the Romantic Movements in Europe. The Romantic Movement in American literature might date from 1819, when Washington Irving's *Sketch Book* appeared, to 1854, the date of Thoreau's *Walden*. Before that period a few Gothic Tales had appeared like *Count Roderick's Castle* in 1795 and the six novels of Charles Brockden Brown written between 1798 and 1801. They were all reflections of English literature rather than American.

There was one American writer, whose school days were spent in England, but who had an individual style and who had a definite influence on European Romanticism, especially the French Romantics, and he was Edgar Allan Poe. His first poem, *Tamerlane*, was published in 1827 and from then until his death in 1849 he produced many masterpieces of romantic poetry and prose. In verse he had a singularly lyric style which made *The Raven, Bells* and *Annabel Lee* so beautiful. In prose he had a lurid, morbid and eccentric imagination which made his short stories like *The Fall of the House of Usher* and *Murders in the Rue Morgue* unforgettable.

Poe was the most typically romantic writer in the United States. Irving might be considered the next, but he lived so much in Europe and was so influenced by his surroundings that he never seems completely American. Nevertheless, his first work, *The Sketch Book*, in which he gathered together the legends of the Hudson Valley and the Catskills, is a romantic work in the same sense that Tieck's collections of German folk songs or Grimm's fairy tales were romantic. Also, many of the legends have a strong romantic flavor, as the headless rider which frightened Ichabod Crane in the *Legend of Sleepy Hollow,* and the story of *Rip Van Winkle.* Hawthorne and Cooper might also be called Romantics, for they turned to the past for inspiration, the one to the early history of Massachusetts and the other to the Indians.

Bryant was the best known poet, excepting Poe, of the period. He, like Wordsworth, turned to nature for inspiration. Thoreau might be called a Romantic because of his Walden experience, his insistence on the rights of the individual and his sincere love of the outdoors.

In the writings of the succeeding generation of American authors the best known of whom are Whittier, Longfellow and Emerson, there are many traces of romantic thought. Romanticism is still discernible in American literature. A striking example is *Tristram* by E. A. Robinson.

There is no distinguishing feature of the Romantic

Movement in the United States, unless it be an interest in local legends and history, which is a characteristic of the Movement everywhere, but because of the lack of other traits is more noticeable in American literature.

The Romantic Movement in literature was not confined to these four countries, but appeared also in Spain, Italy, Scandinavia and the other countries of Europe. Naturally, if there was a movement in literature of such importance, it had its origins in a changing attitude toward all phases of existence, which change may be traced back to England in the seventeenth century.

Classicism has been defined as continuous growth; romanticism as the love of change. The classic temperament shows itself in contentment with existing conditions. The romantic temperament betrays itself in dissatisfaction. The dissatisfaction of the Romantic period expressed itself most forcibly in political revolutions in almost every country except England, and not even England was free from discontent in the first half of the nineteenth century. The English were not content with the Poor Laws, the Corn Laws, the representation in Parliament and the Anglican Church. They did not have a revolution, but they did have the conflict over the Reform Bill of 1832 and the Chartist Movement. The reason that England did not have a revolution in the Romantic period is that she had had her revolutions earlier, in the seventeenth century. The English had expressed their dissatisfaction with the Catholic Church and autocratic government in their treatment of the Stuarts by beheading one and deposing another.

This political experimentation in seventeenth-century England naturally produced a literature of political theory to justify events. John Locke in his *Two Treatises of Gov-*

ernment was the most successful apologist. He adopted the social-contract theory [25] and added that if the government no longer fulfilled the purposes for which it was created, then the people had a right to dissolve the government by revolution. These ideas were completely at variance with the divine right of kings theory which Bishop Bossuet was clearly enunciating at the same time in France.

On the continent, in the seventeenth century, people were generally willing to accept the prevalent notion that supreme power came from God. In England they were demonstrating that supreme power lay in the will of the people. Toward the end of the century, the English example and ideas were beginning to spread on the continent. The French philosophers adopted and transformed the English notion of the rights of the individual to spiritual, intellectual and political freedom. The French ideas in turn spread eastward and in large measure were responsible for the paternal humanitarianism of the Enlightened Despots.

Unfortunately, in France, where the advanced, liberal ideas were so prevalent among the literati, the Court remained conservative and autocratic. Madame de Pompadour was one of the most liberal members of the Court of Louis XV, but her position was too perilous to enable her to become a reformer. Necker, in the next reign, understood the situation, but was powerless to stem the dissatisfaction which, owing to bad harvests and heavy taxes, had become widespread. Therefore, in France, there were the opposed elements of the self-complacency of the Court and the discontent of the people. When, finally, the Estates

[25] The first thorough exposition of the social-contract theory in England appeared in 1594 in *The Laws of Ecclesiastical Polity* by Richard Hooker.

General were called in 1789, the idealists felt that order
and content could be restored by legislation. The people
were not so farsighted, but were hungry for revenge, which
was satisfied in Paris by the Reign of Terror.

The armies of the French Revolution, trained by Carnot
and animated by love of country, a country where each
man had a chance to become important, became invincible
before the mercenaries and the spiritually apathetic
armies of the Holy Roman Empire. With the conquests of
the Revolutionary armies went the ideas which had animated the Revolution, and discontent spread throughout
Europe. The same ideas went with the conquests of Napoleon and grew to defeat him. The ideal of freedom became
important, and it was soon evident that it could not be
achieved under Napoleonic control. The people of Europe
turned against Napoleon, but had no desire to restore their
former governments. The Napoleonic fiasco was so sudden
and so complete, however, that the conservatives, the
trained veterans of the old school, had their innings at the
Congress of Vienna. Nevertheless, the seeds of discontent
had been planted, and manifested themselves throughout
the century.

The dominating attitude of the Romantic period was
discontent and love of change. It showed itself not only
in politics and literature, but also in art and music, in costumes and manners.

Architecture is the most conservative of the arts, but not
even it was free from the romantic spirit and the love of
change. The love of change does not necessarily imply a
desire for something new, but is content with something
different. So it was with the architecture of the period.
There was a reaction against the late Renaissance styles

which were to be found in every country in Europe and America in the eighteenth century. But no new style was created; instead there were revivals of former styles, and above all of the Greek and the mediaeval.

The Greek style was associated in men's minds with the democracy of Athens and so was akin to the political aspirations of the period. The mediaeval styles were connected with the former greatness of each country. Each country claimed the Gothic style of architecture for its own, which explains why the non-partisan misnomer, Gothic, has persisted. Goethe and Friedrich Schlegel wrote of *die deutsche Kunst*. Horace Walpole spoke of the English style. Alexander Lenoir had a museum of *l'art français*. The vogue for the mediaeval was in harmony with the growing nationalism of the period.

The present study is concerned only with the Gothic Revival and the literature of the Romantic Movement which aided its vogue.

CHAPTER II

THE BEGINNINGS OF THE GOTHIC REVIVAL IN ENGLAND

GOTHIC REVIVAL is the term given to modern buildings designed in a mediaeval style. The term was first used in England about the middle of the last century. By 1870, when Charles Eastlake was writing his history of the Gothic Revival, the term had become part of the English language. By the end of the century, it had become a generally recognized name for a definite style of architecture. It is interesting to notice that there is no similar term in any other language. That is not surprising, for although modern Gothic has been built in almost every country, the revival began and became most important in England.

One reason for this may be that the mediaeval styles never completely died out in England, but have been occasionally used ever since the Tudor period. Not many examples are known to have been built in the seventeenth or the first half of the eighteenth century; but even Sir Christopher Wren tried his hand at designing Gothic.

Just what Wren's opinion of the Gothic was has been variously interpreted. We know that he did use it, not only in Oxford, but also for seven parish churches in London and that years of his career were devoted to restoring, repairing and adding to mediaeval buildings such as Ely, Westminster and Salisbury. It seems as if this excerpt from the *Parentalia* gives certain insight into his attitude. "We

22

now most esteem the Learning of the Augustan Age, yet, no question there were then many different styles in Oratory, and perhaps some as good as Cicero's. This is not said as any Inducement to Masons, or every Novice that can draw lines, to fall into crude Gothick Inventions, far from the good examples of the Ancients." [1] That he could be sympathetic to Gothic is shown by his comments on Salisbury. "As this Church is justly esteemed one of the best patterns of Gothick-building, a short Architectural Account therefore may bespeak the Attention of the Curious as a further Taste of that Style of Architecture." He speaks well of the "first Architect, whose judgment I must justly commend for many things, beyond what I find in divers Gothick Fabrics of later Date, which, though more elaborated with nice and small Works yet want the natural Beauty which arises from the Proportion of the first dimensions." [2]

Wren has often been scorned for his theory of the origin of the Gothic style, but the recent work of the French archaeologist, Dieulefoy and in the past decade of Lavedan make it seem that perhaps Wren was not so mistaken. "This we now call the Gothick Manner of Architecture (so the Italians called what was not after the Roman Styles) though the Goths were rather Destroyers than Builders; I think it should with more Reason be called the Saracen Style; for those People wanted neither Arts nor Learning; and after we in the West had lost both, we borrowed again from them, out of their Arabick Books, what they with Great Diligence had translated from the Greeks. The Crusaders gave us an Idea of this Form. The Saracen mode of Building seen in the East, soon spread over Europe and

[1] *Parentalia*, p. 289.   [2] *op. cit.*, p. 304.

particularly in France; the Fashions of which Nation we affected to imitate in all Ages, even when we were at Enmity with it." [3] Wren recognizes the priority of the French which was not acknowledged for more than a hundred and fifty years after his time. He had, however, no notion of the organic structure of Gothic and instead of eulogizing the buttresses which permitted the lofty vaults and the pinnacles which weighted down and stabilized the outer buttresses, he was quite scornful of them. "Pinnacles are of no Use and as little Ornament." "Nothing was thought magnificent that was not high beyond Measure, with the Flutter of Archbuttresses, so we call the sloping Arches that poise the higher Vaultings of the Nave." [4]

No new architectural style springs upon an astonished world like Athena from the head of Jove. Since architecture is the most practical and utilitarian of the Fine Arts, it is the most conservative. To produce a new style, a new popular taste, new social requirements and new materials must precede the change. The Gothic Revival was no exception; almost a century was required to bring about the changes necessary to make modern buildings in mediaeval styles acceptable to the patrons of architects in the nineteenth century.

To trace the origins of any movement is a fascinating but often futile task. Nevertheless, causes are a great preoccupation of historians. Causes of wars are often grouped

---

[3] *op. cit.*, p. 298.

[4] Clark, *Gothic Revival*, p. 7, quotes a sentence from the *Parentalia* of which he writes, "I see no reason to doubt that it represents Wren's true sentiments." If he had looked again, he would have noticed that that particular sentence is quoted from John Evelyn, who was always more fervently Italian than Wren. (*Parentalia*, p. 308, from Evelyn, *Account of Architecture*, p. 9.)

under the headings remote, indirect and immediate and the same divisions may be used for the Gothic Revival.

The remote cause of the Gothic Revival is the change in taste which occurred in the eighteenth century. In the seventeenth century Inigo Jones and Christopher Wren introduced into England the late Renaissance style of Palladio. In the early eighteenth century a purer Roman style became popular owing particularly to the patronage of the third Earl of Burlington. His house at Chiswick, planned by Campbell and Kent, and the gardens ornamented with vases and statues from Hadrian's villa at Tivoli set the fashion which was refined and perfected by the Adams brothers in the middle of the century. The classic architecture was but one manifestation of the vogue for the classics which dominated the Augustan Age which began the eighteenth century. But by the end of the century a reaction had begun and some people were growing weary of the formality of the classic styles and the more individual and ornate mediaeval styles were growing in favor. The change in taste goes from the Palladian to a more eclectic one. In writing of the Gothic Revival there is a great temptation to be interested in every evidence of mediaevalism and to consider it important, but many histories of architecture are written without mentioning it and others sum up the movement in an unflattering paragraph. In the eighteenth century there was certainly a change in taste which was indirectly responsible for the nineteenth-century revival of mediaeval styles, but it led even more to eclecticism than to the predominance of any one style.

However, since this work is on the Gothic Revival, it shall be concerned especially with the mediaevalisms of the eighteenth century which changed popular taste. These could be discussed under the three headings antiquarian, literary and architectural, but since the three aspects often fuse in the works of one man, it seems best to treat the subject chronologically.

An Englishman who died in 1704 is very largely responsible for the change in taste which came about in this century. His name was John Locke and he disregarded the long-held theory of innate ideas. He said that the mind of a child was a *tabula rasa* on which experience wrote; and the mind of man was the sum of his experiences.[5] It was, therefore, important how each individual was educated and trained to use his eyes and hands, for the only source of knowledge was the senses. To a great extent Locke was instrumental in bringing about the increased interest in nature and the abandonment of classical spectacles which made the Augustan Age see beauty only in the classic mold.

Joseph Addison was a younger contemporary of Locke and is often cited as one of the most classic writers of the reign of Queen Anne. He was a versatile man and well travelled. He made the grand tour of Italy in his youth and wrote letters commenting on what he saw. When he was in Pavia, he wrote of the Certosa as follows, "Their church is extremely fine, and curiously adorned, but of a Gothic structure." [6] He felt that it would be improper to be too enthusiastic about any building not in the classical manner, and most especially the Gothic. The word Gothic had been used in the English language since at least 1642 when it is found in the diary of John Evelyn. It was taken from the Italian and used in the same manner to describe any archi-

---

[5] Cf. Thomas Aquinas. *Nihil est in intellectu, quod non fuerit prius in sensu.*

[6] G. W. Greene, *Works of Addison,* II:152.

tecture which was not classical and therefore barbarous and devoid of taste. The word was often used as a synonym for crude, rude, rough and uncouth. Addison uses the word about thirty times in his writings and usually as a term of opprobrium. But he did not scorn all literature that was not classical in form. He wrote of English ballads several times in the *Spectator* and admired particularly *Chevy Chase*. He also recognized the merit of Spenser and enjoyed the *Faerie Queene*.

Addison died in 1719, and Alexander Pope is the great literary light of the 1720's. He is generally considered the Augustan or classicist, par excellence, of English literature. He translated the Odyssey and the Iliad in heroic couplets, which were his favorite style of poetic utterance. His poetry is full of pithy and witty lines, which have been so often quoted that they have almost become proverbs—as for instance:

"Hope springs eternal in the human breast." [7]

His *Essay on Criticism* and *Rape of the Lock* are equally quotable. Despite his verse form, his love of the classics and his interest in his contemporaries, a careful reading of his poetry shows that he had read with attention Spenser, Shakespeare, Milton and Dryden and some of the native romanticism of English poetry is discernible even in his rigid poetry.

"What beck'ning ghost, along the moonlight shade
Invites my steps, and points to yonder glade?"

Pope was not a forerunner of the Gothic Revival, but even he could appreciate the art of the Middle Ages, al-

[7] *Essay on Man*, Epis. I, l. 95.

though his comments in the following letter are moralistic as is the way of classistic writers. "In the Hall is one vast arched window, beautifully darkened with divers scutcheons of painted glass: one shining pane, in particular, bears date 1286, which alone preserves the memory of a Knight, whose iron armour is long since perished with rust, and whose alabaster nose is mouldered from his monument. The face of Dame Eleanor, in another piece, owes more to that single pane than to all the glasses she ever consulted in her life. After this, who can say that glass is frail?" [8]

Toward the end of the decade James Thomson was composing his poems which were collected under the title *The Seasons* and published in 1730. He was the first of the Nature Poets and the popularity of his work led to an increased interest in nature and counteracted the effect of the graveyard poetry which had a certain vogue in the '30's. In the next decade Collins's *Odes* and Young's *Night Thoughts* strengthened the fashion which was reacting against the classic style of Pope and enjoying a more personal, contemporary expression of poetical emotion.

The first man who could be definitely called a forerunner of the Gothic Revival was Batty Langley, who with his brother Thomas published several books in which the Gothic style was considered. The Langleys were moderately successful architects of the second quarter of the century. They put up many buildings, very few of which are still standing. They would probably be completely forgotten if they had not written books which are still referred to in architectural courses and which are to be found tucked away in dark corners of a few architectural libraries. They are seldom read today, but they must have been more pop-

[8] *Pope's Works,* Warburton's Edition, Vol. VII, p. 346.

ular at the time, for there were three editions of the work which is of special interest to the Gothic Revivalist.

The title page of the second edition of 1747 reads as follows: *Gothic Architecture improved by rules and proportions In many grand designs of Columns, Doors, Windows, Chimney-Pieces, Arcades, Colonnades, Porticos, Umbrellos, Temples and Pavillions, Etc. with Plans, Elevations & Profiles; Geometrically Expressed.* The short title by which the book is generally known is *Gothic Architecture Improved.* It has caused devout mediaevalists with a sense of humor much delight, but the others have been irritated and have showered abuse on Batty Langley.

Very little is known of the Langley brothers, except their works, the titles of which are very informative: *A Sure Method of Improving Estates,* 1728; *New Principles of Gardening,* 1728; *The Builders Compleat Assistant, or a library of arts and sciences absolutely necessary to be understood by builders and workmen in general,* 1738; *The Builder's Jewel,* 1741; *The Builder's Director, or Bench Mate: A Pocket-Treasury of the Grecian, Roman and Gothic Orders of Architecture, Made easy to the meanest Capacity by near 500 Examples, Improved from the best Authors, Ancient and Modern etc.* Perhaps the most delicious is the following: [9] *Ancient Architecture restored, & Improved, by A Great Variety of Grand & useful Designs, Entirely New in the Gothick Mode For the ornamenting of Buildings & Gardens. Exceeding every Thing thats Extant Exquisitely Engraved on LXIV large Quarto Copper-Plates and printed on Superfine Royal Paper.*

This last work gives great insight into the knowledge of

[9] This is the title of the first edition of 1742, the second edition of which was *Gothic Architecture Improved,* 1747.

018459

mediaeval architecture in the middle of the eighteenth century. Langley, although greatly criticized, was a respectable working-architect with a genuine interest in mediaeval architecture, and the first to use or adapt the style since the vogue for classical architecture had swept England in the 1660's. His attitude and his knowledge were different from ours today as several passages from the last work show.

Ancient Architecture, restored and improved has two dedications. The first is to Charles, Duke of Richmond, and John, Duke of Montague; a paragraph of which runs as follows: "The Encouragement of Arts and Industry being Your Grace's Delighte, and this Specimen (or Attempt) for to restore the *Rules* of the ANCIENT SAXON ARCHITECTURE, (vulgarly, but mistakenly called *Gothic*) which have been lost to the Public for upwards of seven hundred Years past, being *Honoured* with Your Grace's *Approbations*, and *Encouragements;* It is therefore most Humbly Inscribed to Your Graces Protection." The style is typical of the century with the lavish use of capitals and italics. There are three statements which must be commented upon. First that Batty Langley felt that there were rules of ancient Saxon architecture. At the present time there is a strong feeling that mediaeval building was done by rule of thumb, by trial and error and experiment, that there were no set rules to work by as there were in the classical and Renaissance periods when the works of Vitruvius, Alberti, Palladio, Serlio gave rules for the construction of buildings. Batty, however, was so impregnated with the classic tradition that it seemed inconceivable that any architecture should be without canons, and since he could find none for the Gothic, he tried to make some. In *Gothic Architecture Improved* he evolved five orders of Gothic architecture, doubtless hoping to be a second Vitruvius, but instead he has been considered a presumptuous fool.

The second statement to be noted is that he wished to substitute the term Saxon for Gothic, and the third that this type of architecture, or rather the rules for it, have been lost for about 700 years, which would be since 1040 A.D.

The second dedication is to the Dean and Chapter of the Collegiate Church of St. Peter, Westminster; in which he says: "Your Venerable and August Piles, being the most Magnificent in this Kingdom (and the almost inimitable Structure in the World) of the *Saxon Mode*, (though vulgarly called Gothic) as well as the most renowned . . . and as by strict researches I have discovered many of the Rules, by which its principle parts are proportioned and adorned . . . I have illustrated their uses . . . in private Buildings, in the same *mode*, which was never done or attempted before and as such may justly be esteemed an Improvement in the noble art of Building" he humbly dedicates the work. Later in the work he says that to make authentic his forty-two original plates, he has added two drawings of columns in Westminster Abbey, which give a notion of his "strict researches."

Then follow the names of "Encouragers to the Restoring of the Saxon Architecture." The list begins with the name of Hardwick, the Lord Chancellor, next fifteen Dukes, twenty-six Earls, including the fourth Earl of Shaftesbury, three Viscounts, two Bishops, Winchester and Rochester, twenty Lords and a miscellaneous group of forty-nine names including Right Honourables, Ladies, Justices, a carpenter and a mason and also the name Horatio Walpole who most probably was the future builder of Strawberry Hill. That makes a total of 116 influential people whom Batty Langley could persuade to subscribe to his book.

Then comes "A Dissertation on the Antiquity of the Principle Ancient Buildings that have been, and now are in this kingdom, by Way of Introduction to the following Work." He begins by lamenting that the rules of this ancient architecture are lost. "Upon the strictest Enquiry into the History of this kingdom and into Chronicles of past ages, it doth not appear that any Edifices were built by the Goths in this kingdom: Notwithstanding, that every ancient Building, which is not in the *Grecian Mode* is called a *Gothic Building*." He gives a brief history stating that "in 449 the Romans left Britain after being here 500 years." "Then Hengist and Horsa, Saxons came." "In 530, the Saxons were masters of the first four kingdoms of the Heptarchy." "Edmund in 1017 was the last of the Saxons. Therefore Saxon should be the name of the buildings." "We know nothing of Buildings standing when the Saxons came after the Romans left, nor is it possible we should, since the art of Printing was then unknown." "In 597 Christianity first was introduced among the Saxons." "Saxons built towns but Danes burnt them down." "By this unhappy Conquest (the Danish), Posterity was deprieved, not only of the Saxon Modes or Orders of Architecture, but in general of the Geometrical Rules by which Buildings were set out and adorned." Still bothered by the term Gothic, he concludes that the Picts and Jutes were Goths. "Now I have shown that the Posterity of the Goths by their Union became English Saxons." These Goths who became Saxons built magnificently from about 600 to the Danish conquest when all the buildings were destroyed by the Danes. " 'Tis therefore evident, that none of the ancient Buildings now standing in this Kingdom which have been erected since the Danish Conquest are real Gothic (or Saxon) Buildings, as they are commonly called."

The first part of his dissertation tries to show the fallaciousness of calling non-classical buildings Gothic and to show why they should be called Saxon. The second part is a list, with comments, of "The Principle Buildings erected from the Beginning of the Danish Monarchy in 1017 to the reign of King James the first, when Inigo Jones lived, who I think was the first Person that introduced Grecian Architecture in England." He has high praise for the Henry VII chapel and wished that the secret of the building had been transmitted "and it could have since printing had started." He ends the list with the Banqueting House, Whitehall (1603–1635). "Now as it is very reasonable to believe that the Modes in which all these Buildings have been erected, the Banqueting Hall excepted, were taken from fragments found among Saxon ruins, they may therefore be called Saxon Buildings but why they have been called Gothic, I cannot account for." But custom is too strong, so he concludes by saying, "But they have been called Gothic and I shall continue to use the term."

From an historical angle Batty Langley is most interesting, for it is generally agreed today that what we call Gothic architecture was first built in the second half of the twelfth century and became a fully fledged style in the thirteenth century. We now feel quite sure that the Saxons before the Danish conquest built no edifices in the Gothic style. We have now clearly distinguished between the Saxon and Gothic architecture. In English we are no longer troubled by the misnomer Gothic. The French scholars, being purists, have tried to abandon the term and to use instead *l'art ogival* or *l'art français,* but they, like Batty Langley, have had to accede to the usual term, Gothic. We all know that Gothic art appeared long after the Gothic kingdoms had been lost in the history of Spain and Italy, and the Goths had nothing to do with that method of construction. Langley, however, felt that if the art was called Gothic it should have originated with the Goths. He did not realize that "gotica" meant barbarous, and the sixteenth-century Italians thought that everything not in the classic tradition was barbarous and so started the use of the term Gothic for non-classical buildings.

There is also a positive side to the importance of Batty Langley. About 1750 there was a wave of Gothicism which spread into all the minor arts in England. It was not long-lived, nor a major style, and the phase of the Gothic Revival of the 1750's which we are best acquainted with is the Chippendale Gothic. In almost every museum there are examples of that style of furniture. In chinaware the vogue was reflected in the Staffordshire designs of ruined castles and abbeys. Today we do not often see the Gothic wallpaper and hangings which were popular then, nor the silverware with Gothic curlicues. The designs and publications of the Langleys aided the architectural side of this vogue.

The Langleys were not the only ones to use Gothic. William Kent, who designed everything from palaces to ladies' costumes, was one of the first to employ Gothic in the eighteenth century. On February 27, 1738, he submitted a design for the courts of Chancery and King's Bench on the Dais of Westminster Hall, in which he used ogee arches and pinnacles, which design was accepted and built. Another architect who had great skill in making Gothic designs was Sanderson Miller, who from 1744 to 1760 was well occupied making sham ruins and Gothical garden pieces and even a church, although his most excellent work is the Palladian town-hall in Warwick.

This vogue for the Gothic was not confined indoors, but could also be seen in the gardens. The picturesque grew in popularity throughout the century. Early there was a re- action against the formal English garden with its prim box hedges and clipped trees. Even Addison objected to the severity of the English gardens and when on his travels in France and Italy found their gardens more untidy and in- formal and consequently more pleasing. He wrote to Con- greve in 1699, "I am however so singular as to prefer Fon- tainebleau to all the rest. It is situated among rocks and woods that give you a fine variety of savage prospects." [10] In the *Spectator* No. 414 he wrote, "There is something more bold and masterly in the rough careless strokes of nature, than in the nice touches and embellishments of Art." These sentiments became more prevalent as the dec- ades went on. Everyone who could tried to have "a fine variety of savage prospects" and "an artificial wildness." William Kent was kept busy designing new gardens and Lancelot "Capability" Brown was much in demand. The eighteenth-century English garden was a true expression of the Rococo, or as it is generally called in England, the Picturesque. William Shenstone is the man who best ex- presses this fad. In 1745 he began transforming his farm, called Leasowes, into an artificial wilderness with vistas and a "ruinated priory," a temple of Pan made of rough, unhewn stone; a statue of a piping faun and another of the Venus de Medici beside a vase of goldfish.

[10] Greene, *op. cit.*, II:463.

Shenstone was but one of a host of garden enthusiasts. "Commonsense" as early as 1739 wrote of them in *The Gentleman's Magazine.* "Everyman now, be his Fortune what it will, is to be *doing something at his Place,* as the fashionable phrase is: and you hardly meet with any Body, who, after the first Compliments, does not inform you, that he is *in Mortar* and *moving of Earth:* the modest terms for Building and Gardening." [11] But even those who had no estates were interested in the gardens of others. John Wesley, for instance, was a great amateur of gardens and whenever he had time he visited nearby estates and wrote descriptions of them in his diary, using all the appropriate phrases of a man of taste. Wesley visited Leasowes in 1782 and writes of it, "I never was so surprised. I have seen nothing in all England to be compared with it. It is beautiful and elegant all over. There is nothing grand, nothing costly; no temples, so called; no statues; (except two or three, which had better have been spared;) but such walks, such shades, such hills and dales, such lawns, such artless cascades, such waving woods, with waters intermixed, as exceed all imagination!" [12] Only in Ireland at New-Dargle did he see anything comparable. "I have not seen so beautiful a place in the kingdom; it equals the Leasowes, in Warwickshire, and it greatly exceeds them in situation; all the walks lying on the side of the mountain, which commands all Dublin-Bay, as well as an extensive and finely variegated land-prospect." [13]

That Gothical garden pieces were built is corroborated by another description which Wesley gives of an Irish

[11] *The Gentleman's Magazine,* IX:640, Dec. 1739.
[12] Wesley, J., *Journal,* Everyman ed. IV:237.
[13] *op cit.* IV:397.

estate. "I went with a few friends to Lord Charlemont's, two or three miles from Dublin. It is one of the pleasantest places I have ever seen: the water, trees, and lawns, are so elegantly intermixed with each other, having a serpentine walk running through a thick wood on one side, and an open prospect both of land and sea on the other. In the thickest part of the wood is the Hermitage, a small room, dark and gloomy enough. The Gothic temple, at the head of a fine piece of water, which is encompassed with stately trees, is delightful indeed; but the most elegant of all the buildings is not finished: the shell of it is surprisingly beautiful, and the rooms well contrived for use and ornament. But what is all this, unless God is here? Unless he is known, loved and enjoyed? Not only vanity, unable to give happiness, but 'vexation of spirit.' " [14]

These gardeners were not scornful of Batty Langley, but were glad to order a Gothic Umbrello to terminate a view, a summerhouse or a ruin. Batty Langley's designs were eagerly perused by the amateur gardeners; and he did many Gothical garden pieces, before his death in 1751.

It is not surprising that Batty Langley has no reputation today, for even his contemporaries spoke slightingly of him. He caused a small Gothic vogue among the fashionable, but there was another group composed of Gray, Walpole, the Wartons, Hurd and Mason who were also interested in the Middle Ages and considered themselves superior to Batty's bastard Gothicisms and their attitude is still with us.

The most important of the group, the one who knew most and had the best discernment, was Thomas Gray. On August 13, 1754, he wrote to Thomas Warton: "You do

[14] *op cit.*, IV:134–5.

not say enough of Esher. It is my other favorite place. It was a villa of Cardinal Wolsey's of which nothing but a part of the gateway remained. Mr. Kent supplied the rest, but I think with you that he had not read the Gothic classics with taste or attention. He introduced a mixed style which now goes by the name of the 'Batty-Langley manner.' He is an architect, that has published a book of bad designs." [15] Mr. Gray may be scornful of Langley, his mixed style, and book of bad designs; but he has also some strange ideas according to our notions. We speak of country houses, not villas; we call sixteenth-century architecture Tudor not Gothic; and we know of no Gothic classics which Mr. Kent might have read with taste or attention.[16] Nevertheless it is an interesting quotation for it gives us a notion of Gray's opinion of Langley's Gothic style.

A month later Gray again wrote to Warton: "I rejoice to find you at last settled to your heart's content, and delight to hear you talk of giving your house some Gothic ornaments already. If you project anything, I hope it will be entirely within doors; and don't let me (when I come gaping into Coleman Street) be directed to the gentleman's at the ten Pinnacles, or with the church porch at his door."[17] This gives some notion of the popularity of Gothic decoration and the way that it was used.

Gray and Walpole were at Cambridge together. After they went down, Walpole had to make the Grand Tour befitting a prime minister's son and he invited Gray to accom-

[15] Gosse, *Gray's Works,* II:253.

[16] Mr. Whibley in his recent edition of *The Correspondence of Thomas Gray* thus comments: "Gray means that Kent had not studied the classical examples of Gothic Architecture." Vol. I, p. 404, footnote 12a.

[17] Gosse, *op. cit.,* II:254.

pany him. Gray accepted and they started off in September 1739. They both wrote amusing letters which have been printed. Walpole was the man of the bon ton, while Gray was the reflective observer. It is amazing that such different temperaments got along as well as they did. The great interest of Gray's letters is that, so far as we know, he was the first English traveller to enjoy and admire the continental cathedrals.[18] Of Notre-Dame at Rheims he wrote: it has a "beautiful Gothic front with two towers of surprising lightness." [19] In his letter to his mother, he gives a good description of Amiens. "We have seen the cathedral, which is just what Canterbury must have been before the Reformation. It is about the same size, a huge Gothic building, beset on the outside with thousands of small statues, and within adorned with beautiful painted windows, and a vast number of chapels, dressed out in all their finery of altar-pieces, embroidery, gilding and marble." [20]   From Siena, he again writes his mother. "What it has most considerable is its Cathedral, a huge pile of marble, black and white laid alternately, and laboured with a Gothic niceness and delicacy in the old fashioned way." [21]   In his letters there are many other references to Gothic architecture which show that he did not scorn the style but was genuinely pleased by it. His interest in the Gothic did not wane on his return to England but remained one of his major interests all through his life. In his Journal in the Lakes of 1769 there are various references, for in his late years he tried to make notes on all the Gothic buildings in England so that he could more closely differentiate styles.

[18] Daniel Defoe in c.1724 admired English cathedrals, especially Lichfield.
[19] Gosse, *op. cit.*, II:28.   [20] *Ibid.*, p. 18.   [21] *Ibid.*, p. 64.

Gray was also interested in the origins of the style and in 1754 wrote an essay on Norman Architecture which was formerly attributed to Bentham. In it he tries to clear up the Saxon problem and justly decides that the early Gothic came in with the Norman conquest and so suggests that name. He gives as the origin of the pointed arch the explanation which has since been so often used, that is the intersection of round arches. It was the first work which showed an archaeological approach to mediaeval architecture.

Other phases of the Middle Ages interested him also and he studied Norse and read Welsh translations of early sagas. These studies bore fruit in his poems: *The Bard* written in 1755, and even more in the *Fatal Sister* and the *Descent of Odin*. His influence may not have been widespread, but it was great on his narrow circle of friends.

Horace Walpole was one of Gray's friends who was most affected and who in turn affected popular taste. Walpole at heart was a classicist, but his dilettante tastes were stronger even than his classic tastes. He was a rich man, the son of a powerful prime minister, he held several government positions which netted him a good income, he was a bachelor and prided himself on being a man of taste. He had many friends and acquaintances to whom he wrote excellent letters. Taking the notes and the outline of Mr. George Vertue he wrote *Anecdotes of Painting* in which he publicly acknowledges his debt to Gray for reading over the manuscript and making corrections. Gray's enthusiasm for the Gothic may have been influential in his decision to make Strawberry Hill a Gothic edifice. He bought the original house in 1747 and gradually enlarged and gothicized it between 1753 and 1776.

Strawberry Hill is the most famous of eighteenth-century attempts at the Gothic. Often all the works of the century are grouped together under the name "Strawberry Hill Gothick." It is not used with an intent to flatter, for the post-Viollet-le-Duc mediaevalists shuddered when they found buildings which pretended to be in the Gothic manner and yet were not stone vaulted, but were constructed in the simplest manner like a cardboard box and then plastered over with pinnacles and crockets and a few pointed arches. They considered this heresy to the great constructional art of the Middle Ages.

On June 8, 1771, Walpole wrote a friend: "I have made a Gothic gateway to the garden, the piers of which are of artificial stone, and very respectable. The round tower is finished, and magnificent; and the state bedchamber proceeds fast, for you must know that the little villa is grown into a superb castle." [22] It is remarks like that about the "artificial stone" and "very respectable" which show that Walpole was living in the century of Batty Langley. Appearances were what really counted in the eighteenth century and nowhere is that more clearly shown than in their use of the Gothic. Nevertheless, Strawberry Hill became a great show place and Walpole complained that the tourists were taking away bits as souvenirs.[23]

Walpole was very proud of Strawberry Hill and asked various of his French friends what they had heard of it. They were not flattering. M. de Guisnes said that he had heard that it was all lath and plaster and very uneven. Mme. du Deffand said that it was only what could be expected from a country which had not achieved true taste. Which reminds me of the contemporary epigram:

[22] Mason, *Horace Walpole's England*, p. 219.   [23] *Ibid.*, p. 453.

"The French have taste in all they do,
Which we are quite without:
For Nature, which to them gave goût,
To us gave only gout." [24]

Thomas Gray was quite polite about Strawberry Hill when he was feeling friendly toward its owner and wrote a friend, "I am glad you enter into the spirit of Strawberry castle. It has a purity and propriety of Gothicism in it (with very few exceptions) that I have not seen elsewhere." [25] But another time after Walpole had made a short call on Gray when their relations were rather strained, Gray sat down and wrote, "Mr. Walpole hurried home in the evening to his new gallery, which is all gothicism, and gold, and crimson and looking glass." [26]

As Kenneth Clark says, "Walpole gave Gothic social standing." [27] The style had been in vogue since the '40's and about 1758 the Rustic Music House at Vauxhall had been rebuilt in the Gothic mode, but the best families had considered it a parvenu style, but when the fastidious and aristocratic Walpole turned his country place into a Gothic mansion, the style could no longer be snubbed. Walpole did more than to make the style acceptable to the élite. He felt himself to be a student of the Gothic and was eager to have authentic models for his gates, doors and fireplaces. The chimney in the Holbein Chamber he said was taken chiefly from the tomb of Archbishop Warham at Canterbury. Walpole emphasized the archaeological tendency of the Gothic Revival which became so strong after 1820.

The decade of the 1760's witnessed the publication of a

[24] By Thomas, Lord Erskine, 1728–1823, in *English Epigrams and Epitaphs*, p. 94.
[25] Gosse, *op. cit.*, II:255.
[26] *Ibid.*, III:150.
[27] Kenneth Clark, *Gothic Revival*, p. 72.

number of works which aided the growing interest in the Middle Ages. The only architectural work of importance was the remodeling of Strawberry Hill. It was the literary works which were influential. I have already mentioned that Gray had become interested in Erse poetry and published the *Fatal Sister* and the *Descent of Odin* in 1761. They have the wild, occult, and grim character which became associated with the Middle Ages. Thomas Warton published an essay on the *Faerie Queene* which heightened the appreciation of the symbolic, mystical character of the mediaeval period and also gave authority for the non-classical poetical forms.

Bishop Warburton wrote an essay on the origin of the pointed arch. He still felt that there must be some connection with the Goths and suggested that when they settled in Spain they evolved the new style which was then taken over by the Moors and Saracens and from them adapted by the builders of western Europe. Thomas Gray wrote critically of this essay, "that the Gothic manner is the Saracen or Moorish, he has a great authority to support him, that of Sir Christopher Wren, and yet (I cannot help thinking) is undoubtedly wrong." Their buildings "seem plainly to be corruptions of the Greek architecture, broke into little parts indeed, and covered with little ornaments, but in a taste very distinguishable from that we call Gothic. There is one thing that runs through the Moorish buildings and imitators would have tried to copy, that is the Cupola—yet who ever saw a Gothic cupola? I do not see anything but the slender spires, that serve for steeples, which may perhaps be borrowed from the Saracen minarets on their mosques." [28]

Richard Hurd, bishop of Worcester, in 1762 published

[28] Gosse, *op. cit.*, II:257–8.

twelve *Letters on Chivalry and Romance*. In letter VIII
he writes, "When an architect examines a Gothic structure
by Grecian rules, he finds nothing but deformity. But the
Gothic Architecture has its own rules, by which when it
comes to be examined, it is seen to have its merits as well as
the Grecian." [29] These letters were widely read and had a
great importance for they showed that there were two different but equally important styles of writing, the classic
and the romantic. He pointed out the merits of each and
their different principles of composition which were as dis-
similar as Grecian and Gothic architecture and emphasized
that they had to be judged by their own standards.

Horace Walpole decided that he must add to the growing
literature inspired by the Middle Ages, so in June 1764 he
retired to compose, with his tongue in his cheek, *The Castle
of Otranto, a Gothic Tale*. It was published immediately in
1764 and was very popular. It started a school of prose
writers which continued until 1820 and gave a new meaning to the word Gothic. The story is short but full of horror
and sensibility, baronial halls, trapdoors, a cloister, a suit
of armor, plumes, plentiful sprinkling of blood, injured
innocence, tyrannical usurpation of power, young love,
messages, faithful servants and honest peasants, a duel and
a sepulchral voice, tears, fainting fits, beauty and stalwart
courage. These are a few of the mise-en-scène which Walpole brilliantly wove together to produce the first Gothic
Tale. This tale of horror added another overtone to the
adjective Gothic which was gradually substituted for its
earlier meaning of barbarous and uncouth. Gothic came to
signify something wondrous, supernatural, weird, strange
and out of the ordinary.

[29] Hurd, *Works*, IV:296.

There were three other publications of the '60's which must be mentioned, for although they did not deal with architecture or the Gothic, nevertheless, by their popularity they greatly enlarged the reading public which became conscious of the Middle Ages.

Bishop Percy published a collection of ballads in 1765 entitled *Reliques of Ancient English Poetry*. He was not the first Englishman to be interested in English ballads; Samuel Pepys had collected in manuscript about 2,000 ballads and Percy made use of his collection. Addison in the *Spectator* (No. 70, 74) had written appreciatively of ballads, but Percy was the first to publish a group and so make them available for the general reading public. He was more than a casual antiquarian with literary tastes: he was a scholar of some depth and from his footnotes one can gather that he was acquainted with the French historical writings of Mallet, Pelloutier, Rapin and Le Grand, as well as with the chronicles, and Tacitus, Bede and the English historians. The three volumes contain poetry of various periods, few, but the most famous, are earlier than the sixteenth century from which there are a great number including a sonnet by Queen Elizabeth and some are as late as the eighteenth. The introductory essays are interesting. In volume one he writes on the "Ancient Minstrels"; in the third volume on the "Ancient Metrical Romances"; in the second he is concerned with the origins of ancient poetry. He mentions Bishop Hurd as an "elegant writer" and then tries to disprove his theory of the origins of Gothic literature by pointing out that the subject matter of the Metrical Romances goes back far behind the Crusades and Chivalry for its inspiration. Percy also discredits Moorish and Spanish influences and emphasizes instead the Danish and

Frankish origins of ancient poetry. The *Reliques* were widely read and enhanced the growing reputation of the Middle Ages.

The next year saw the publication of a book which really caused a furor. It came out under the patronage of Horace Walpole which insured a wide circulation. It was edited by a Scotchman named Macpherson and was called *Fingal* by Ossian. Fingal was a traditional Celtic hero of the third century and Ossian, his son, was supposed to have written of his great deeds, and Macpherson, the canny Scot, was supposed to have found fragments of these poems of which he made prose translations. Men like Gray and Percy questioned the authenticity of this work and it was soon recognized to be a forgery. Walpole was rather put out by the whole affair and got rather caustic when he wrote to Horace Mann in 1775, "To return to Ossian: is it not evident that the Scots are of Irish parentage? Hurt at the charge of having never produced a *poet*, they forge an epic in *prose?*" [30] Despite his forged character, Ossian immediately became popular and retained his fame for fifty years. It was not so much the poems and prose transcriptions as the atmosphere and the heroic manner of life which appealed to the eighteenth-century imagination. Macpherson supplied a new adjective, "Ossianic," which vied with Homeric in popularity. Ossian and his tales of Fingal and Temora typified the chivalric side of the tribal society of the early Germanic and Celtic barbarians. Anything which was wild, picturesque, brave or generous was Ossianic and his vogue spread quickly into France, where he became a favorite of Napoleon, and into Germany, where Goethe admired him.

[30] Mason, *op. cit.*, p. 248.

The last important figure of the decade was Thomas Chatterton, who died in 1770 at the age of eighteen. His writings were not so influential in themselves but more because of his personality, his tragic end, and the controversy which grew about them. Chatterton was the posthumous son of the sacristan of St. Mary Radcliffe at Bristol. His mother was poor but was able to send him to a charity school and then apprentice him as a scrivener to a Mr. Lambert in Bristol. His forebears had long been connected with the church of St. Mary, and his father in 1750 had cleared out some of the manuscripts which had been stored in a room in the tower of the church. The old parchment had been used by the Chatterton family for wrapping paper. The precocious boy early studied the history of Bristol and realized the worth of these parchments which were about the house. By the age of fifteen he had learnt that there was a fifteenth-century clerical writer of Bristol, named Rowley. It is now generally agreed that all the writings which Chatterton produced as being by this Rowley were forgeries, but they were sufficiently well done to cause a controversy over their authenticity. There were also drawings which purported to be from the hand of Rowley, many of which were of Bristol castle, which was begun in 1138. The sketches exhibited a most mongrel style of architecture which could not be called twelfth-century nor possibly even of 1440 in which year Rowley was supposed to have made the drawings. Even the eighteenth-century critics found it difficult to accept ionic capitals on the engaged columns and the drawings appeared more similar to a Batty Langley design than anything else.

Chatterton was amazingly precocious and wrote with some wit and occasional wisdom on a number of topics. He even wrote an essay on Sculpture, perhaps inspired by Walpole's success with the *Anecdotes of Painting*. After a brief survey of antique sculpture, he sums up the work of the mediaeval period in a sentence. "The Gothic sculpture sprung afterwards from a wild imagination, unassisted by nature."

Before going to London, Chatterton tried to obtain the patronage of Horace Walpole, but the latter, made wary by his experience with Macpherson's poems, did nothing more than answer him civilly. Walpole received much criticism for his neglect of Chatterton, especially after he poisoned himself. Walpole in writing to Mann in 1779 said, "I believe McPherson's success with Ossian was more the ruin of Chatterton than I. Two years passed between my doubting the authenticity of Rowley's poems and his death. I never knew he had been in London till some time after he had undone and poisoned himself there." [31]

Chatterton's short, tragic life and his intense preoccupation with the Middle Ages affected the imaginations of his contemporaries and even more the later romantic poets all over Europe. He helped to enlarge the growing interest in the Middle Ages. And in reading of him and his friends, like Mr. Catcott, one gains a slight insight into the widespread antiquarian interest in the provincial towns.

Many books were published in the last quarter of the century which illustrated ancient monuments and gathered together information about them. One of the first of importance was the history of Ely cathedral by James Bentham published in 1771. Bentham was a friend of Gray and early a Gothic enthusiast. Grose got out a series of Antiquities between 1773 and 1795 which had a great sale and

[31] Mason, *op. cit.*, p. 265.

increased the general appreciation of ancient monuments. In 1786 Carter had printed *Specimens of ancient Sculpture and Painting* and nine years later *Ancient Architecture of England*. He made excellent drawings and was engaged to prepare illustrations for the *Builder's Magazine* and to do etchings for the Society of Antiquaries. He was an ardent advocate of the Gothic, and was troubled not only by the neglect of ancient buildings but also by the haphazard methods of restoration which were employed. In *The Gentleman's Magazine* between 1798 and 1817 there appeared 211 letters signed "An Architect" which discuss the proper method of restoration and which are generally considered to be Carter's.

Not all the works were antiquarian but some were practical also. The most important of these professional books was that gotten out by Wallis in 1774 and called the *Carpenter's Treasure,* in which all the information was gathered together in a serviceable and simple fashion. A much later work that was of great use to the builders was Joseph Halfpenny's *Gothic Ornaments in the Cathedral Church of York,* published in 1795.

Two works published in 1798 must be mentioned. One was by Bentham and Wallis, *History of Gothic and Saxon Architecture in England* and the other was by Bishop Milner, *History of Winchester.*

The Gothic remained fashionable in fiction; Clara Reeve and Mrs. Radcliffe were two of the most successful followers of Walpole in the writing of Gothic Tales. Their novels were full of horrors and so were those of Lewis, who wrote the *Monk,* Maturin and a host of other writers whose popularity continued until about 1820.

The journals, but most especially *The Gentleman's Mag-*

azine, testify to the growing popularity of the Gothic, and
not only in architecture but all phases of life in the Middle
Ages. Therefore, it is not surprising that many of the nobility and the landed gentry followed Walpole's example
and had their houses Gothicized. In 1780 Asbury was
Gothicized by Sir Roger Newdigate. About the same time
Sir William Chambers worked on Milton Abbey, and even
Robert Adam who is best known for his use of the classical
style was employed by the Duchess of Northumberland to
make her a Gothic interior. One of the best known buildings was that called Lee Priory (it had nothing to do with a
priory but the name sounded romantic) built for Thomas
Barrett in Kent in 1782 by James Wyatt. Walpole praised
it highly for it purity of taste. At least eleven others which
were built about the same time suggest that the vogue for
the Gothic was growing.

James Wyatt (1746–1813) should certainly be mentioned as one of the forerunners of the Gothic Revival. He
did a great deal of work and most of it in the Gothic manner. Walpole wrote to Mann as early as 1775, "Wyatt, less
fashionable, has as much taste, is grander and more
pure." [32] By the '90's Wyatt had become the most fashionable architect in England. He was employed on a great
number of restorations and the nineteenth century abused
him roundly. He worked at Durham, Lichfield, Winchester, Salisbury and the Henry VII chapel at Westminster.
He did so much restoration that churchwardens used his
name automatically in connection with any new work and
he got abuse for a great deal that he never did.

His most spectacular work was Fonthill Abbey built between 1796 and 1799 for William Beckford, the author of

[32] Mason, *op. cit.,* p. 249

Vathek. Fonthill was the whim on a gigantic scale of a wealthy dilettante. He had inherited a perfectly good Renaissance house from his father, but he felt that his genius was stifled in such a conventional dwelling, so he demanded a Gothic mansion befitting his flights of imagination. It was a spectacular showplace with a high central tower and an enormous hall and indoor staircase and was the climax of eighteenth-century Gothic. Beckford soon tired of it and sold it in 1819 to a Mr. Farquhar. At the same time he sold his collection. How much interest was taken in Fonthill may be judged from the fact that 7,200 catalogues were sold in a few days at a guinea each. Soon after the sale Beckford learned that the workmen had neglected the foundations in order to finish the superstructure on time. When Farquhar heard this he said calmly that "It will last my time," but he was mistaken, for during a gale one winter night of 1823 Fonthill Abbey collapsed "without a noise." Beckford some time before his death in 1844 was asked what part he had played in starting the Gothic Revival. He replied that he could never blame himself for that.

George IV decided that if Gothic dwellings were becoming so popular, he might as well have something done to his authentic Gothic palace at Windsor. It was in a very dilapidated state and had to be almost completely done over and made to conform to the prevalent idea of a Gothic castle. The younger Wyatt, a nephew of James, was employed to oversee the alterations. He added the Hundred Steps which lead from the river side and added the bastions and crenellated walls which now make Windsor a typical mediaeval castle. George IV was so pleased by the work that the architect was elevated to Sir Jeffrey Wyatville.

Many country gentlemen looked with interest at the

restorations at Windsor, and a great number of them decided that they would like to live in little Windsors with
miniature bastions, towers and machicolations and crenellated walls. The architects were busy putting up country
houses in this style, which has since received the name
castellated. The Reptons, father and two sons, and Smirke
were considered the best architects for this type of house in
England; and Gillespie and Crichton in Scotland, and the
two Morrisons in Ireland. Castellated country houses
dotted England in the early years of the nineteenth century.

In the early years of the nineteenth century there was a
reaction in literature against the eighteenth-century Gothic,
particularly against the Gothic Tale of Horror, which was
still popular as is shown by the numerous editions of Mrs.
Radcliffe's novels, Maturin's and Lewis's. Jane Austen
(1775–1817), that marvel of female literary genius, was
one of the first to see the absurdity of the fantastic, over-
sentimental novels, and her first works made gentle fun of
them. The first was *Sense and Sensibility,* which carica-
tured the fainting, sensitive heroines; the second, a much
more mature work, *Northanger Abbey,* showed what too
much reading of the *Mysteries of Udolpho* would do to an
otherwise sensible young girl. Catherine Morland is invited to stay in an old house and she is certain that there
must be a ghost and old parchments, but all she finds are
the laundry bills of the last guest, and when she goes in
search of the haunted room she runs into her host, Charles
Tilney, who has to disillusion her and assure her that the
house, although old, has no mysterious history.

Another writer who amused himself at the expense of the
devotees of the Gothic was Byron. Don Juan goes to an old
English house at the end of his travels and thinking to find

a ghost on the ramparts, finds instead, "The phantom of her frolic Grace-Fitz-Fulke." He also has a few satirical comments to make on the craze for castellated country houses. Part of two stanzas from *Don Juan* must be quoted:

> "To Norman Abbey whirl'd the noble pair,
> An old, old monastery once, and now
> Still older mansion,—of a rich and rare
> Mix'd Gothic, such as artists all allow
> Few specimens yet left us can compare." [33]

Another one well expresses the prevalent opinion of restorations.

> "There was a modern Goth, I mean a Gothic
> Bricklayer of Babel, call'd an architect,
> Brought to survey these grey walls, which though so thick
> Might have from time acquired some slight defect;
> Who after rummaging the Abbey through thick
> And thin, produced a plan whereby to erect
> New buildings of correctest conformation,
> And throw down old, which he call'd restoration." [34]

The tide might be turning against the eighteenth-century expressions of mediaevalism, the Gothic tale and the Gothic country house, but the interest in the Middle Ages was growing stronger every year. In the first decades of the nineteenth century the poems and novels of Sir Walter Scott did signal service for the Gothic Revival in making the Middle Ages so pleasant and attractive. Ruskin says that his knowledge of history came from reading the novels of Scott. The picture of the Middle Ages found in Scott was in the mind of every Gothic Revivalist. Jane Porter, who wrote *The Scottish Chiefs* in 1808, claimed to have

[33] Byron, *Don Juan,* Canto XIII, stanza LV.
[34] *Ibid.*, Canto XVI, stanza LVIII.

started the vogue for the historical novel and accused Scott of plagiarism and not giving her due credit. It is true that from 1814 the Waverley Novels overshadowed her works.

Scott was a Scotch lawyer with literary and antiquarian interests. He gathered all the legends and history and fragments of the Middle Ages that he could find and wove them into living novels. He was not archaeological in his studies and had very vague notions of the different styles of Gothic architecture. The Gothic Revivalists criticized his inaccuracies, and especially his baronial hall at Abbotsford which presented a mongrel style. Ruskin, when he was a young man, went north to look at Abbotsford and was deeply shocked by the architecture which showed that Scott had no real knowledge of the Gothic or pure archaeological appreciation of it. His architectural knowledge was more akin to that of his predecessors, Langley, Walpole and Beckford, than to that of the Gothic Revivalists. But he did a great deal for them, for he popularized and made bearable the Middle Ages and so helped form a public which would accept the more archaeologically correct buildings of the nineteenth century. He swept away the disagreeable idea of the Middle Ages which the Gothic tales had made prevalent. He took the Middle Ages from the misty, murky and uncomfortable past and peopled them with honest, human characters, who seemed life-like and understandable. He took away the heroic qualities of Fingal and substituted more everyday characteristics. He made history a popular subject, and what is more, a readable one. It was not difficult to read *The Monastery* and *The Abbot,* and almost everyone did. Scott's poems and novels reached even the lower middle class and so molded public opinion of the Middle Ages that it was ready to accept the Gothic Revival.

In these pages, I have tried to mention the people, buildings and books which were most influential in changing popular taste in the eighteenth century and up to 1820 when the ideals of the Gothic Revival began to be formulated. The eighteenth century was as complex as any other, although often it has been called the classical century par excellence. The more we study it, the more aspects are discernible. I have tried to emphasize those which lead from the classical supremacy to the mediaeval. There were not just the two attitudes, but from 1750 on there was a growing electicism of taste which culminated in the late Victorian period. The Chinese had a vogue. The excavations at Pompeii and Herculaneum and the publications of Sir William Hamilton had their reflections in current taste. The publication in 1762 of the *Antiquities of Athens* by Stuart and Revett had as much influence on taste and architecture as these Gothicizing books and buildings. Nevertheless in this eclecticism, there is one strong tendency which may be followed through the century and which bore fruit in the Gothic Revival: that is the growing interest and knowledge of the Middle Ages and Gothic architecture.

Chapter III

THE GOTHIC REVIVAL IN ENGLAND

THERE WERE several events in the social and economic history of England which helped to make the Gothic Revival possible in the nineteenth century. The most important of these was the growth of population. In 1740, London had a population of 725,000, by 1800, 864,000 and by 1891 over four million. There were only 15 cities in England in 1801 with a population of over 20,000 which totalled about one and a half million people. By 1891 there were 185 English cities of over 20,000, with a combined population of over 15,500,000. The total population of England and Wales in 1801 was not quite nine million, but by 1891 it had increased over three times to more than twenty-nine million.[1] These few figures give a notion of the great increases not only in population but also in towns. New towns and increased population require new churches.

Exactly what was responsible for the growth of population is difficult to determine, but more hygienic conditions and better food may have decreased the death-rate. The growth of towns and urban population is easily accounted for, however, for it was directly dependent upon the Industrial Revolution which changed England from an agricultural country to a manufacturing one. In the nineteenth century England led in the manufacture of textiles. At first the spinning and weaving was done in the cottages of

[1] A. F. Weber, *Growth of Cities*, pp. 43–46.

the workers, but as elaborate and expensive machinery was introduced it became necessary to build factories and have all the workmen employed under one roof. The people were then forced to live near the place of work and so the industrial cities of Birmingham, Manchester, Leeds and Sheffield grew in size.

The Industrial Revolution not only concentrated population and so caused a need for new churches, but it also produced new building materials which to some degree aided the Gothic Revivalists. Especially important was the increased production of iron which enabled the builders to use an iron skeleton on which to build their vaults and arches and so insure a more stable construction.

The need for new churches was soon recognized by the government; as early as 1818 an Act of Parliament had been passed for building and promoting the building of additional churches, and a Royal Commission had been appointed for carrying the Act into execution. By 1830 one hundred and thirty-four churches had been built by the Commission and fifty were under construction. There was no attempt at architectural refinement in these structures, but economy and durability were stressed. Few of these buildings were in the Gothic style, but references are found in the reports to "Roman of the Tuscan Order" and "Grecian Doric with Cupola." These buildings were later known by the half contemptuous name of "Commissioners' Churches" and are of little architectural value, but serve to show that there was a genuine need for ecclesiastical buildings.

At the same time there was an Incorporated Society for Promoting the Enlargement, Building and Repairing of Churches and Chapels which got out pamphlets to instruct builders and masons. These emphasized durability and convenience, and had a word about the style, recommending Gothic, adding that "the Grecian Doric is also eligible."

Another event which was important in the background of the Gothic Revival was the religious awakening of the Anglican Church brought about by the Oxford Movements, that of Wesley in the eighteenth century, and that of Newman in the nineteenth. At first glance these Movements might seem to have weakened rather than strengthened the Church, for although Wesley remained Anglican until his death, his followers left the Church to form the Methodists, and the leader of the second Oxford Movement left the Episcopal Church to become a Roman Catholic. It was the religious fervor of these men and their followers which was communicated to the members of the Church of England and helped to make it the important and living sect that it is today.

A superficial survey of England in the eighteenth century leads one to the conclusion that religious fervor was not fashionable. Some of the Dissenters were fervently religious and there were many sects, for as Voltaire remarked, "An Englishman, as one to whom liberty is natural, may go to heaven his own way," [2] but he continued by saying that for professional preferment, it is necessary to belong to the Church of England. "This reason (which carries mathematical evidence with it) has converted such numbers of dissenters of all persuasions, that not a twentieth part of the nation is out of the pale of the established church." [3]

And many members of the Church were apathetic or

[2] Voltaire, *Letters Concerning the English Nation,* p. 27.
[3] *Ibid.*

even hostile to revealed religion, for it was the age of Deism and Skepticism. Pope wrote of churchgoers—

"Some to church repair,
Not for the doctrine, but for the music there." [4]

Voltaire, after commenting upon the religious enthusiasm of the Cromwellian period, wrote, "But the people are now so very cold with respect to all things of this kind, that there is little probability any new religion, or old one that may be revived, will meet with favor." [5]

The success of John Wesley, Whitefield and the Evangelicals in the latter half of the century shows that Voltaire underestimated the latent religious feeling in England.

Nevertheless, Wesley, himself, comments upon the lack of religious enthusiasm in some of his contemporaries. The reading of Dr. Robertson's *History of America* led him to remark upon it. Of the book, he wrote, "I suppose his History is preferable to any History of America which has appeared in the English tongue. But I cannot admire . . . a Christian Divine writing a history, with so very little of Christianity in it. Nay, he seems studiously to avoid saying anything which might imply that he believes the Bible." "It is true, the doctrine of a Particular Providence (and any but a Particular Providence is no Providence at all) is absolutely out of fashion in England; and a prudent author might write this to gain the favour of his gentle readers. Yet I will not say, this is real prudence; because he may lose hereby more than he gains; as the majority even of Britons to this day retain some sort of respect for the Bible." [6]

[4] Pope, *Essay on Criticism*, pt. II, l. 142.
[5] Voltaire, *op. cit.*, p. 38.   [6] Wesley, *Journal*, July, 1781.

However one judges the religious temper of England, the Wesleyan revival was a stirring challenge to the more conservative churchmen, and the Church of England, especially in the 1840's, eagerly took up the challenge and this interest in religion aided the interest in church building and hence the Gothic Revival.

The growth of population, the new materials, the building of churches and the religious revival all played into the hands of the Gothic Revivalists who used them to further their cause of Gothic architecture, but in themselves none of these events promoted Gothic architecture or the interest in the Middle Ages. If a growth of population and a religious revival had occurred a century earlier, the new churches would have been built in the classic or late Renaissance styles like those of Sir Christopher Wren which dot the city of London. But this need for churches combined with eighty years of growing interest in the Middle Ages made the Gothic Revival possible.

The year 1820 is usually given for the beginning of the Gothic Revival, although, as we have seen, buildings had been erected in the Gothic mode since 1740. But it was the picturesque and the romantic which had inspired these ruins, summerhouses, cottages, villas and castellated country places. After 1820 the criterion of a modern building done in the Gothic manner becomes the archaeological, which is the basic ideal of the revivalist and explains why so many of his buildings are aesthetically displeasing.

Two publications made this archaeological ideal possible. The first was that of Thomas Rickman, who in 1819 brought out a work entitled *Attempt to Discriminate the Styles of English Architecture*. The introduction contains a brief survey of the Five Orders of Vitruvius which reminds us that classic architecture was still popular. The main part of the work is concerned with the architecture in England from the time of the Conquest to the Reformation. Rickman pointed out that the only architecture to be called Saxon would be that built before the Conquest and that none built afterwards could be so named. He suggested Norman as the fit term for the buildings erected directly after the Conquest by the Norman conquerors and then divided the so-called Gothic into the three main styles. Early English was the name which he gave to the work of the thirteenth century; Decorated to that of the fourteenth; and Perpendicular to that of the fifteenth. The names were almost universally accepted and it then became possible to differentiate the styles of mediaeval architecture. What the general term should be was still a question. "The un-adventurous suggested 'Pointed'; the pretentious 'Plantagenet'; the pious 'Christian'; the official and self-assertive 'English.' " [7] The younger Pugin used Christian, but by his death in 1852, Gothic was the generally accepted term. What Rickman did, once and for all, was to distinguish the three main styles of mediaeval English architecture and so give the archaeologists terms with which to work.

The other work was of especial value to the practicing architect who wished to design in the Gothic manner. This was the *Specimens of Gothic Architecture* (1821) by Pugin and Willson. Many books of plates had been issued illustrating the beauties of the ancient architecture in England, but the universal desire had been to make a picturesque plate showing the romantic setting of the monument so that it would appeal to the sensibilities of the fair perusers. Many of them were charming and some were excellently

[7] Kenneth Clark, *Gothic Revival*, p. 89.

done, but they were of little use to the architect who wished to design an archaeologically correct Gothic doorway. In this work every specimen was drawn to scale with geometric cross sections of every molding and crocket. As Eastlake remarks, "For the first time the structural glories of Westminster Hall were revealed with mathematical nicety; the graceful mouldings of York and Lincoln were accurately profiled on a large and intelligible scale; . . ." [8] It made an invaluable handbook for the architect who wished to be exact in his copies of Gothic architecture. From then on it was possible to have imitations and exact copies instead of new inventions in the Gothic mode.

It was the elder Pugin who made the drawings for this work with the help of his students. His Christian name was Augustus, and he was a French émigré with a talent for drawing. He had no money when he arrived in Ireland, but early entered the office of Nash who vied with Wyatt as the most popular architect of the Regency. Nash did a great number of the Commissioners' Churches and so had a great deal of work to depute to the men in his office. He had little aptitude for making Gothic designs but found that Augustus Pugin was very skillful in the Gothic. After some years Pugin started an office of his own and trained a number of young men in the rudiments of architecture. The most famous of his pupils was his son, A. Welby Pugin, who became an ardent revivalist. The other was Ferrey, who did some Gothic Revival work which was well regarded in his day, but who is mostly known now for his Memoirs of the two Pugins. The elder Pugin did a number of drawings which were engraved by Le Keux, the best of the architectural engravers of the day.

[8] Eastlake, *History of the Gothic Revival*, p. 88.

E. J. Willson, who wrote the text in the *Specimens of Gothic Architecture,* had as great a knowledge of architecture as was possible in his day. His clear, lucid introduction and excellent description of the plates aided greatly in making these volumes a turning point for the Gothic Revival.

The publications of John Britton must be mentioned, also. He did not die until 1856 when the Gothic Revival was in its prime. He was born in 1771 when Walpole was building at Strawberry Hill. His works form the link between the picturesque works of Grose and the archaeological works of Whewell. He produced about seventy volumes of drawings of mediaeval architecture, which, although they were not geometrically exact like Pugin's, nevertheless were much more accurately drawn than the former works of the same type, and so sharpened the public eye and made it aware of the different styles of mediaeval architecture and so more able to appreciate the copies of the Gothic Revivalists. The first of his books was the *Beauties of Wiltshire,* the fruit of a three months' walking tour. It was an immediate success, and so followed the *Beauties of England and Wales* series which appeared between 1800 and 1816 in eighteen volumes. Commercially it was a great success. As early as 1805 Britton sensed the coming change from the picturesque to the archaeological and so started the series entitled *Architectural Antiquities of Great Britain* which appeared in forty quarterly issues, ending in 1814. He found that the public appetite for illustrations of mediaeval architecture was not satiated, so he started the series of *Cathedral Antiquities* which appeared almost yearly until 1835. One reason for the great vogue of Britton's publications was that they served as illustrations to the novels of Sir Walter Scott. Britton provided the visual side of the Middle Ages, while Scott gave the human side. At all events, after the public had looked at the seventy works edited by Britton, it was impossible to ignore the Gothic style of architecture.

Eastlake sums up the opening years of the Gothic Revival by saying, "an age of ignorance was succeeded by an age of plagiarism." [9] He adds that the copies were generally better than the originals which occasionally the architects tried to design.

At the back of his book, Eastlake gives a list of 343 buildings which he considers to have been the best examples of the Gothic Revival style done before 1870. He begins his list with St. Luke's, Chelsea, a church designed by J. Savage in 1824 in the perpendicular style. His remark about it is, "The earliest *groined* church of the modern Revival." It was much admired when it was built. *The Gentleman's Magazine* praised it highly and gave it the compliment of using a picture of it for a frontispiece and the subject for the leading article in March 1826. They regretted, however, that the style chosen was eclectic perpendicular, when Early English was both purer and more national. The church is still standing and has a certain charm with its tall tower and thin flying buttresses. Eastlake comments that it has a dry style and a mechanical look, but to us now that is more pleasing than the very ornate Victorian Gothic.

During the 1820's and '30's there were many architects using mediaeval styles. Savage and Ferrey we have already mentioned. Some of the best known of the others were Shaw, Blore, Buckler, Poynter, Tite, Salvin, Scoles and Burton. Sir Charles Barry in 1826 designed the church of

[9] *Ibid.*, p. 89.

St. Peter's at Brighton in the Middle Pointed style. The mediaeval style was not restricted to churches but also used for colleges and rustic cottages or lodges on large estates. The general aim was toward more archaeological correctness. "At last it seemed necessary to find precedent for every detail, and, to quote the humorous hyperbole uttered by a well-known member of the profession, no one was safe from the critics, who knew to a nicety the orthodox coiffure of a thirteenth century angel and who damned a moulding that was half an hour too late." [10]

Naturally the picturesque attitude toward the use of Gothic did not disappear overnight. Kenneth Clark thinks that it lasted on until 1845, and that the Parliament Buildings were the last expression of it. Thomas Rickman, who differentiated the styles so successfully, was by no means a purist. In 1822 he designed St. George's Church in Birmingham which Eastlake praises in restrained terms as an excellent building save for one unfortunate solecism. "The window tracery is remarkably good in motive, but, sad to say, is all executed in cast iron." [11] The later revivalists always found it difficult to excuse the use of iron, although it seems very logical to use the new material which was structurally good. Rickman's Gothic at Cambridge is more interesting, for it so well illustrates the pre-revival use of Gothic. St. John's College needed more rooms, so a New Court was built between 1827–31 and designed by Rickman. It was placed across the Cam and connected with the rest of the college by the so-called Bridge of Sighs. There were no other buildings along the Backs to obscure it and so the building was planned with a pleasing façade and a late Gothic cupola. It was designed to be the fitting

[10] *Ibid.*, p. 137.   [11] *Ibid.*, p. 93.

end of the vista along the Backs, to terminate a view. The sides are faced with stone but decorated with less Gothic tracery than the front. The back is a plain brick wall, now painted gray, with a few plain sash windows, completely undecorated. It looks like a factory or prison and has no hint of the Gothic which so tastefully decorates the front. Appearances still counted for more than the principles of Gothic construction.

The religious revival of the '30's and various societies united to put a new conscience in the architects who worked in the mediaeval styles.

We can barely realize what a state of perfunctoriness the Church of England was in at the beginning of the century. The services were performed with apathy and the buildings were neglected. Cathedrals were turned into museums or shut up completely. A book entitled *The Broad Stone of Honour* describes the conditions in 1824. In 1832, Arnold wrote, "The Church as it now stands, no human power can save."[12] But from then on there was a change. In July 1833 Keble gave his famous assize sermon on National Apostasy and Newman at Oxford began writing his *Tracts for the Times*. Pusey started the High Church movement. Suddenly there was a wave of interest in the Church and an earnest desire to make her a more vital part of modern life. Newman and his group, Isaac Williams, Manning, Froude, and Keble, author of the *Christian Year*, have often been called the Tractarians. This group aided the Gothic Revivalist by holding the conviction that the old forms of worship, which seemed to them more reverential and heartfelt, could be brought back only if the old type of architecture could be revived, so they eagerly advocated

[12] Kenneth Clark, *op. cit.*, p. 194.

the use of Gothic for ecclesiastical buildings. By 1845, when Newman was received by the Church of Rome, the Tractarians had broken up, as their way of thinking diverged, but the *Tracts for the Times* had done their work and all England was more sensitive to the forms of religious observance, as well as genuinely more interested in moral questions and the ethical aspect of architecture. The Roman Church bore the fruit of the movement in the conversions of Newman and Manning, but the main interest and enthusiasm which it aroused was concentrated in the Church of England.

By 1840 it was possible for a Protestant archaeological scholar to write, "The most important requisite in erecting a church is that it be built in such a way that the Rubrics and Canons of the Church of England may be consistently observed and the Sacraments rubrically and decently administered." [13] That meant that ritual and sacraments were coming back to their own. The strong aversion to any ceremony which savored of Rome was vanishing.

The societies which played an important role in changing the plans of churches and the service were in no way connected with a church organization, although a great many of their members become churchmen. There were already established the Society of Antiquaries in London, the Archaeological Society in Oxford and the Antiquarian Society in Cambridge. These were all preoccupied by the Gothic and engendered in their members an appreciation of mediaeval architecture and history.

These societies were not enough and others were founded. The most important of these new organizations was the Cambridge Camden Society founded in 1839 by

[13] *Ibid.*, p. 192.

J. M. Neale and Benjamin Webb. There was already a literary society in London also named Camden, which caused some confusion, but they likewise wished to honor the memory of the great Elizabethan antiquary. T. Thorp was the first president and Dr. Mill, Regius professor of Hebrew, H. Goodwin, P. Freeman, J. S. Hawson, Venables, F. A. Paley, S. N. Stokes, and Beresford Hope were some of the first members. Neale started the campaign for liturgically correct churches by his *Few Words to Church-wardens* which pointed out in forceful manner the disgraceful neglect which the old churches had suffered and gave advice on the building of new churches. It was followed by the *History of Pews* which was a subject of great interest to the revivalists, for, of course, there had been no pews in the Middle Ages, while in the seventeenth century they had become an important expression of snobbery. To have, or not to have, pews was a serious question.

In November 1841 the Society founded a magazine of its own, called the *Ecclesiologist*. The name was their own invention, but within a few years ecclesiology had become a popular topic and the word frequently used. The growing interest in the symbolic aspect of church building became intensified by the publication of a translation of the work of Durandus by the Camden Society. Soon the proper position of the pulpit, the place of the font, the use of the chancel, the addition of a choir screen, the situation of the altar and the subjects used for the decoration of the churches became subjects for great argument. The problem of proper restoration interested them also and one of the first numbers of the *Ecclesiologist* was devoted to the restoration which was being done on the Church of the Templars in the Tower.

This intense interest in symbolism, liturgical fitness and the desire to have restorations in every way conforming to the original Gothic plan, could not but arouse the suspicions of the more Protestant. The most famous criticism of the Camden Society was given in a sermon by Mr. Close in Cheltenham on the fifth of November 1844. It was published, and thousands of copies were sold during the next year. The full title ran as follows: *The "Restoration of Churches" is the Restoration of Popery: proved and illustrated from the Authentic Publications of the "Cambridge Camden Society."* The *Ecclesiologist* tried to answer this and other criticisms, but various members of the Society resigned and others were leaving Cambridge; therefore it seemed wise to move to London and to change the name to the Ecclesiological Society, both of which were done in 1846. The Society continued to grow and its publications to exert great influence. By some inexplicable mystery they were able to divorce Rome from the Gothic and use it as a purely English and Anglican style of ecclesiastical building. The great reason for this was the growing strength of the High Church party. The Society published a *Handbook of English Ecclesiology* which explained the importance of chancels and screens and vestments and plate, and yet dissociated them from the Roman Catholic service. In 1847 they began publishing the series which so greatly influenced the later churches of the Gothic Revival, the *Instrumenta Ecclesiastica*. The *Ecclesiologist* took its mission very seriously and sent out members to look at all of the more important churches which were being built, and if they found anything in the plan which they felt clashed with the true principles of the Anglican liturgy, they either wrote publicly of the errors or wrote privately to the architect informing him of his lapses from the true ecclesiological standards. They were a power to be considered, and were one of the most important factors in the Gothic Revival.

The *Ecclesiologist* was not as one crying in the wilderness. It was merely the most important spokesman. There were many societies with similar ideals. The Oxford Society for Promoting the Study of Gothic Architecture was one. At Bristol, Exeter, York, Lichfield and many other cathedral towns Diocesan or Archaeological Societies were started. They took the place of the local Antiquarian Societies of the previous century and they were very different in purpose and attitude. The antiquarians were interested in any little trifle which they might find. Any part of the past was equally interesting to them, and it was all for diversion. The archaeological societies were more narrow-minded and were usually engrossed by the Middle Ages and spent a lot of time on exact dating; also they supervised the erection of new churches and tried to safeguard this newly recognized ritual of the English liturgy. Religion and Gothic architecture were becoming connected in men's minds.

The greatest landmark of the Gothic Revival is the Parliament Buildings in London. In October 1834 Old Westminster Palace burned down, leaving only part of the old Hall and ruins of St. Stephen's Chapel standing. A Commission was immediately appointed to oversee the erection of new Houses of Parliament. There was a competition for the new plans. The only requirements were that the same site be used and that the style be Gothic or Elizabethan. Tradition and the historical importance of the old palace were responsible for their wish to keep the old site. The style of the old buildings and the Abbey across the street, combined with the patriotic idea that Gothic was the true

English architecture, were sufficient reasons for their choice of style. During 1835 all the leading architects were busy making drawings. Ninety-seven architects presented 1,400 drawings to the jury. In February 1836 they announced that the winning plan was by Charles Barry, a design in the perpendicular style. The ninety-six other architects and their friends were then free to voice their dissatisfaction with the award and the Battle of the Styles commenced. The public took so much interest in the competition that it was decided to hold a public exhibition of all the drawings which had been handed in. Every style was represented— Greek, Roman, Renaissance and Tudor—the public was in general satisfied with the selection of the Commission; but the architects were not. Gothic, as we have noted, had been used for domestic architecture and for churches, but no important civic building had been erected in that style since the time of Inigo Jones.

W. R. Hamilton wrote a series of letters to Lord Elgin during 1836–37 and in these he put forth all the arguments which the Classicists could muster. He felt that Greek architecture was the only pure style and genuinely disliked the Gothic. The Goths had history, tradition and the emotional appeal of the patriotic style and the Romantic Movement to back them. The Classicists had the advantage of a working style, one which was based on theory and practice, but the purely professional attitude could not prevail against the emotional prejudices of the populace and Parliament. They were driven to call the Greek style more in accord with nature, a vague argument and one which could better be used by the Gothicists, who could explain the origin of the Gothic style as being the trees of the forest, with the columns for trunks and the interlacing branches the ribbed vaulting. The Classicists lost out and work was begun on Barry's plan in 1839.

The plan was quite successful. The exterior was particularly fine with the long façade stretching beside the banks of the Thames from Westminster Bridge and the clock tower, which was originally planned to be taller and thinner, but whose present squatter proportions fit in better with the rectangular structure of the main building. He adapted the old hall into an entrance, and designed anew the two main halls for the House of Lords and the House of Commons which he placed centrally, lighting them from the roof, and placing about the various rooms and offices.

It is a successful building, and now vies with the Colosseum and the Taj Mahal as the best known architectural monument in the world, but not all the revivalists were satisfied with it. A. Welby Pugin is quoted as saying, "All Grecian, sir; Tudor details on a classic body." [14] The mention of Pugin brings us to a rather sorry controversy which took place after his death as to who was the art architect of the Houses of Parliament. Filial piety on the part of Pugin's son and undue reticence on the part of Barry were responsible for a duel of pamphlets in the '60's. A. Welby Pugin was twenty-two years old when the Parliament Buildings burned. He was an excellent architectural draughtsman with unusual knowledge of Gothic design, but he had just recently been in jail for bankruptcy, and had entered the Roman Catholic Church. He was in no way fitted to enter a government competition; his age, religion and inexperience were all against him, and he had sense enough to realize it. But he did need money and could draw with extreme facility, and so was hired by two of the com-

[14] B. Ferrey, *Recollections of A. W. Pugin,* p. 248.

peting architects to make their designs. He is supposed to
have said, "Is not this a regular joke? Here are these two
rivals competing for one prize and I am making the designs
for both." [15] He probably did think it a joke, for he did the
drawings for Graham and Barry. About the Parliament
Buildings, Pugin said later, "I could not have made the
plan, it was Barry's own. He was good at such work—
excellent; the various requirements conveyed by the plan,
and above all the Fine Arts Commission would have been
too much for me." [16] And he was undoubtedly right. Sir
Charles Barry was the man for the job no matter what his
designs had been like. It is only fortunate that he chose
such a good ghost. Barry for fifteen years had been one of
the best architects in England and by the time of the competition was middle aged [17] with a great deal of experience.
It is true that his best known work was Italian, like the
Travellers Club (1829–31), but as early as 1826 he had
designed the Gothic church at Brighton. Barry was the
only architect who could deal with the members of Parliament. If the fire had occurred earlier, Wyatt would have
been the man, and if later, Gilbert Scott, but never Pugin.
It is now generally recognized that Pugin did the drawings
and designed all the decoration both exterior and interior.
He designed even ink and paper stands and umbrella jars
in the Gothic manner. Barry did the floor plans and supervised the building, so it seems that in all justice, Barry may
still be called the architect of the Houses of Parliament.
There would have been no discussion at all if Pugin had

[15] E. N. Pugin, *Art Architect,* p. 9.

[16] Trappes-Lomax, *Pugin,* p. 81.

[17] Barry was born in 1795, and was therefore seventeen years
older than A. W. Pugin.

remained an obscure architect's hack, but as it so happened he became one of the most brilliant, prolific and influential architects of the Gothic Revival.

The last sentence may seem too enthusiastic to the people who have never heard of Pugin, and few people have heard his name, although in the past few years he is coming into his own again. The main reason that Pugin has not been known is that he was a Roman Catholic and the Gothic Revivalists of the last century had to be very wary of any connections with the Romish church. The second reason is that Ruskin followed hard on his heels and took over and transformed Pugin's ideas without mentioning him. Lastly, although Pugin designed hundreds of churches, schools and colleges, not one of his buildings is beautiful, but they are simple and in excellent taste, and most are infinitely superior to other Gothic Revival work; none are impressive or breath-taking.

He realized the defects of the buildings which were erected after his designs and two years before he died he wrote, "I believe, as regards architecture, few men have been so unfortunate as myself. I have passed my life in thinking of fine things, designing fine things and realizing very poor ones." [18]

Augustus Welby Northmore Pugin was born on March 7, 1812 and died on September 14, 1852 after doing a hundred years' work in forty. His father was the Augustus Pugin whom we have already mentioned for his geometrical drawings of Gothic architecture. He was educated by his parents, and early showed great aptitude in drawing and special interest in mediaeval architecture, which he felt to

[18] A. W. Pugin, *Some Remarks . . . Relative to Ecclesiastical Architecture,* 1850, p. 11.

be the only beautiful style. He was the only architect of the Gothic Revival who did not have a rigid training in the classic orders.

Pugin was a very precocious child, and by the age of twelve was a good enough draughtsman to assist his father make the drawings for a book on Paris. By the age of fifteen he was employed making designs of Gothic furniture for Windsor. But his first big triumph did not come until he was nineteen, when he made the stage sets for the ballet *Kenilworth* which was presented at Covent Garden in 1831. The scenery really made the opera and gave Pugin ample opportunity to display his knowledge of mediaeval architecture. The next important event was his conversion to Catholicism in 1834, which came, everyone was agreed, as the direct result of his passion for mediaeval architecture. To him the spiritual church which superintended the building of the material church was an integral part of mediaeval architecture which he almost always called Christian and occasionally Pointed. He was passionately fond of the old abbeys and churches; he looked about him and saw no comparable buildings being erected, so he asked why, and the answer seemed clear. When the beautiful buildings were made, the builders were Catholics; now when ugly and unoriginal buildings are built, the architects and workmen are Protestants and indifferent ones at that. That answer was, of course, valid so far as it went, but he interpreted it in what seems to us a very fallacious manner. He had the firm conviction that before the Renaissance and Reformation all Catholics were devout and zealous and that the Christian faith had become utterly debased since those events. It was as painful to him to see Catholic worship in a Greek temple as to see Baptist services in a Gothic chapel. The only solution which seemed possible to him was to restore the Christian faith in its mediaeval form and so to make possible the revival of Christian architecture. These ideas he set forth in a work entitled *Contrasts* which he wrote in 1835 and for which he could find no publisher. Therefore he had it printed at his own expense in 1836, and although he made no money by the venture, he made a name for himself which enabled him to start on his career as a Gothic Revivalist.

At that time he was working as Barry's ghost, but after *Contrasts* many commissions came pouring in from Protestants as well as Catholics. His professional work did not prevent him from publishing a number of books and pamphlets. He had been made professor of ecclesiastical antiquities at St. Marie's, Oscott, and two lectures which he delivered there he printed in 1841 with the title *The True Principles of Pointed or Christian Architecture*. This work had enormous influence and in it he anticipated the functional theory of mediaeval architecture which Viollet-le-Duc made so important.

Pugin begins the first lecture by setting forth the two great rules for architectural design "by knowledge of which you may be enabled to test architectural excellence." "1st, that there should be no features about a building which are not necessary for convenience, construction or propriety; 2nd, that all ornament should consist of enrichment of the essential construction of the building." "Strange as it may appear at first sight, it is in pointed architecture alone that these great principles have been carried out." [19] He then discusses the constructional requirements which necessitated buttressing, vaulting and mouldings in mediaeval

[19] A. W. Pugin, *True Principles*, p. 1.

buildings. The second lecture is a criticism of contemporary buildings in the Gothic manner.

Two years later he published an *Apology for the Revival of Gothic Architecture in England* in which he again criticizes contemporary work and the lack of a definite style in English architecture. He remarks that "private judgment runs riot" and that "Styles are now adopted instead of generated." He is disgusted by the romantic idea that Gothic buildings are "Melancholy—and therefore more fit for religious buildings." He reiterates his belief that "Every building that is treated naturally without disguise or concealment, cannot fail to look well," [20] and that it is only by the resurrection of the true Catholic belief that Christian architecture can again flourish in England.

He also got out a glossary of Gothic ornament which is the only English work that is at all comparable to Viollet-le-Duc's monumental Dictionary. He wrote on ancient plain-song, the present state of ecclesiastical architecture, the present state of public worship among Roman Catholics, and, in 1850, the year of the establishment of the Catholic hierarchy in England, he wrote articles defending it.

The best list of Pugin's work, although it is not complete, is to be found at the back of Trappes-Lomax's life of Pugin. Perhaps the most important ecclesiastical edifice that he designed was the cathedral of St. Chad in Birmingham which was dedicated in 1841. The exterior is simple and well proportioned; the material is red brick with stone facings. The style of the interior is thirteenth century and shows the influence of his European travels, especially in France where he spent several months sketching the cathe-

[20] A. W. Pugin, *Apology*, p. 39.

drals. The piers of the nave arcade are modeled upon those in Amiens, but thinner and more spindly; nevertheless the whole effect is harmonious and the chancel screen is as lovely an example of Pugin's work as is to be found.

The only work which Pugin felt to be worthy of him was his own chapel of St. Augustine at Ramsgate. It is now the church of the Benedictine monks of Thanet. It is a pleasing building, although there is nothing arresting about it. The most pleasing part is the founder's chantry chapel with the tomb of Pugin with his effigy dressed like a mediaeval monk, and statuettes of his three wives and son kneeling in the arcading that decorates the front of the monument.

It is very difficult to see the true significance of Pugin's work, for the Gothic Revival has gone so much further, especially in the United States where the churches of Cram and Goodhue are more the embodiment of Pugin's principles than anything that he built. Still it is generally agreed that the second phase of the Gothic Revival was due mostly to Pugin, who built without resorting to decorations of plaster, cast-iron or papier-mâchée. In the *Apology* he wrote, "We do not want to arrest the course of inventions, but to confine these inventions to their legitimate use and to prevent their substitution for nobler arts." [21] In other words he objected to buying Gothic ornament by the yard and plastering it on to a rectangular construction and then calling it Gothic. He stood for firm solid construction and all the later churches were better for his insistence. He had a genius for designing ornament, but this very ability weakened his power as an architect, for he never was able to build space, which is the highest accomplishment of an architect. Very few builders of the Gothic Revival were

[21] Pugin, *Apology,* p. 41.

able to encompass space until after 1870, for they were too preoccupied with details. Pugin did a great deal for the greater appreciation of Gothic ornament and pointed out the use of plant and flower forms in many of these designs. The full force of his message was somewhat weakened by his romantic and fanatic belief in the Catholic church and the Middle Ages.

The later Victorians whose word had weight with the public did not admire Pugin. Ruskin wrote of him, "he is not a great architect, but one of the smallest possible or conceivable architects." Ruskin did have the grace to add, "I am sorry to have to speak thus of any living architect; and there is much in this man, if he were rightly estimated, which one might both regard and profit by." Some people after the publication of the *Seven Lamps of Architecture* thought that Ruskin had regarded and profited by the works of Pugin. The *Ecclesiologist* in reviewing the book said, "There is much that Pugin himself might learn from this book, if it were not, as is more likely, that Ruskin had learned from Pugin." This charge disturbed Ruskin, and to the third volume of *Modern Painters* he added Appendix IV, "On Plagiarism," in which he owns to having glanced over *Contrasts* in a library and *Remarks on Artists in the Rambler*. . . . He then continues, "I never read a word of any other of his works, not feeling, from the style of his architecture, the smallest interest in his opinions." And in a letter on the same subject, he admits his debt to Carlyle, to Wordsworth, and to others, but winds up with, "But assuredly *Nothing* to Pugin." Whatever may be the truth of the matter Ruskin largely obliterated the memory of Pugin.

William Morris, in a letter of 1876, to his wife, writes that on a walk he had passed "the gim crack palace of

Pugin at Alton Towers." The later mediaevalists thought
Pugin as poor as he had considered his predecessor, "that
scoundrel Wyatt."

Robert Browning sums up the prevalent attitude in a
stanza from *Bishop Blougram's Apology:*

> "It's different preaching in Basilicas
> To doing duty in some masterpiece
> Like this of Brother Pugin's, bless his heart.
> I doubt if they're half-baked, those chalk rosettes,
> Ciphers and stucco-twiddlings everywhere;
> It's just like breathing in a limekiln, eh?"

The name which occurs to most people when the Gothic
Revival is mentioned is that of Gilbert Scott, and that is
not surprising as he was responsible for about a thousand
buildings, twenty-six of which were cathedrals and 476
were churches. He was prolific and popular. There is
barely a town in England where some of his work is not to
be found.

George Gilbert Scott was born in 1811 and trained to be
an architect. His father died when he was twenty-one and
so he was forced to find employment. The Union Work-
house Act was passed at this time so he went about on
horseback canvassing the heads of the unions and getting
them to employ him as architect of the new workhouses. In
1834 he went in partnership with an architect named Mof-
fat and together they erected many buildings which had no
architectural merit. In 1838 he designed his first church,
which was at Lincoln, the commission for which he won in
open competition, and this was followed by six others. According to the lights of the Gothic Revivalists he was still
in the darkness, for these churches were designed without
chancels. But in the next year he read Pugin's *Contrasts*

and became enlightened. He also became aware of ecclesiology by the publications of the Cambridge Camden Society and his whole attitude toward church building was changed.[22]

Scott in his writings describes in graphic terms what Pugin did for him. "I was awakened from my slumbers by the thunder of Pugin's writings. I well remember the enthusiasm to which one of them excited me, one night when travelling by railway, in the first years of their existence. I was from that moment a new man. What for fifteen years had been a labour of love only, now became the one business, the one aim, the one overmastering object of my life. I cared for nothing as regarded my art but the revival of Gothic architecture. I did not know Pugin, but his image in my imagination was like my guardian angel, and I often dreamed that I knew him." [23] Such a passage speaks well both for the influence of Pugin and the sincerity of Scott.

The next year Scott had an opportunity to put into practice these new-found principles in a monument which Pugin greeted with vitriolic pamphlets. This was the Martyrs Monument in Oxford which was erected to the memory of Latimer and Cranmer and Ridley. The Revivalists on the whole were pleased with Scott's design, which was a modification of an Eleanor Cross. He had many more opportunities to put his acquired principles into practice, for he became the leading ecclesiastical architect in England.

His position was strengthened in 1844 by winning the competition for the Lutheran Church of St. Nicholas in Hamburg. It was an international competition and Scott was chosen as the English competitor. He dashed through

Germany drawing a cathedral a day, and on the way home began his sketches for the German Gothic design which was successful. The Gothic Revival had not yet reached Germany and so this design in the national style greatly increased their interest in *die deutsche Kunst*.

Scott did a number of restorations. There is barely a single important cathedral in England which does not bear some marks of his handiwork. His first attempt was at Ely, where he rebuilt the Lantern over the crossing. The proper method of restoration is still a moot question. Scott solved the problem by carefully looking over the building which needed repair, finding traces of the earliest style which had been used there, and then rebuilding in that style. That was his method in parish churches; he was restrained by monetary considerations in cathedrals. It does not seem a good method to us today, but to his contemporaries it seemed excellent, for they and he were both convinced that he built a good Gothic.

In 1856 there was a need for new Government Offices in London, and a competition was held. Scott sent in a Gothic design, which was rejected with those of the other competitors, and a non-competitor was appointed to make the plans. Scott, who had a flair for winning competitions, decided that it was time to write a letter to the *Times,* and the Battle of the Styles raged again. Scott's persuasive powers got him appointed architect, but Palmerston would have no Gothic building. The battle raged back and forth but Palmerston was untouched and insisted on the Italian style. When Scott proved obdurate, Palmerston called for him to say, "I really do think that there is a degree of inconsistency in compelling a Gothic architect to erect a classic building, and so I have been thinking of appointing a coadjutor, who would in fact make the design." [24] That took the wind out of Scott's sails; he accepted the inevitable and tried a Byzantine plan on Palmerston, but he would have none of it, so Scott studied the Italian and produced a satisfactory plan. Scott always cherished his first drawings and used them on the first occasion possible, which was the new St. Pancras station, after looking at which, we may be thankful to Palmerston.

The work for which Scott got his knighthood was the Albert Memorial, built in 1864–72. His conflict with Palmerston over the government buildings had weakened his Gothic morale, and so the monument is a compromise which is often considered to be the most typical expression of Victorian Gothic still extant. It is in the shape of an enlarged mediaeval ciborium decorated with purely Victorian figures.

Scott's most important book was published in 1857 and entitled *Remarks on Secular and Domestic Architecture, Present and Future.* Kenneth Clark calls it one of the most convincing apologies for the Gothic Revival ever written. It restates the principles of Pugin in a more acceptable fashion without the religious bias, and has been a much used and quoted book.

Scott continued working almost without interruption until his death in 1878, and was the most productive of the Gothic Revivalists.

By 1850 the Gothic style of architecture was almost universally adopted for ecclesiastical buildings. The architects of this generation were united by three principles which had been gradually evolving in the past decades. These were archaeological correctness, logical construction,

[24] G. G. Scott, *op. cit.,* p. 190.

and conformity to church ritual. These are the three aims which differentiate the Gothic Revival from the previous building in the Gothic manner.

There were many publications in the 1840's which made these principles universally known and appreciated. In 1842, Professor Willis published an important essay on vaulting in the Middle Ages in the proceedings of the Royal Institute of British Architects, which was significant not only for the erudition to be found in the essay, but also because it shows that the conservative Royal Institute, whose members were generally Classicists, began to recognize the importance of the mediaeval styles of building.

In the same year A. Bartholomew published a book with the lengthy title, *On the Decline of Excellence in the Structure and Science of Modern English Buildings*. It was more popularly written than Willis's essay and was free from the religious bias of Pugin's writings, but combined the main ideas of both writers in deriding the sham building of contemporary architects and insisting on a more logical harmony between decoration and construction, and pointing out the excellence with which the mediaeval architects had achieved this union.

The founding in 1843 of the cheap architectural journal, *The Builder,* was of great aid to the professional architect. The number of articles and illustrations devoted to the Gothic reflect the popular taste and in turn aided in disseminating a knowledge of Gothic styles and especially of the contemporary work done in that tradition.

Not all the publications were for architects. One at least was written for school girls so that they could recognize the main styles of mediaeval architecture and understand the

significance of the various parts of the churches and their
connection with the liturgy of the church. It contained a
few homiletic asides in which the author encouraged the
girls to embroider altar cloths instead of slippers for the
curate. A woman named Miss M. Holmes was responsible
for this book, called *Aunt Elinor's Lectures on Architecture.*[25]

The more purely archaeological interest was continued
by the founding of the British Archaeological Association
"for the encouragement and prosecution of researches into
the Early and Middle Ages, particularly in England."

By the Great Exhibition of 1851, even the poorest and
least educated members of society had an opportunity to
become acquainted with mediaeval styles. This exhibition
was housed in the Crystal Palace, a huge glass and iron construction, designed by Paxton in the manner of a gigantic
greenhouse, and erected in Hyde Park. One of the important exhibitions, despite the fact that the Exhibition was
primarily for industry, was the mediaeval court for which
Pugin was responsible. Thackeray went to the Exhibition
and wrote a humorous poem entitled "The Crystal Palace,"
two stanzas of which are as follows:

> "Say, Paxton, truth,
>   Thou wondrous youth,
> What sthroke of art celistial,
>   What power was lint
>   You to invint
> This combineetion cristial?
>
>   There's holy saints
>   And window paints,
> By Maydiayval Pugin;

[25] Eastlake, *op. cit.*, p. 219.

Alhamborough Jones
Did paint the tones
Of yellow and gambouge in." [26]

There was another event in 1855 which was of greater importance from the architectural point of view. That was the Lille Cathedral competition which was open to anyone throughout the world. It was an important international competition and hundreds of architects competed. The first prize was awarded Clutton and Burges, the second to Street, all English architects. Three silver medals and three "Honourable Mentions" went to six more Englishmen. It was a distinct triumph for the Gothic Revivalists and heightened the prestige of their work. However, it had another effect which was in the end detrimental to the later Gothic Revival. It conclusively proved that the English architects were the most skillful in designing modern Gothic in the middle of the nineteenth century, but it paved the way for the more eclectic designs of the second half of the century. Since the 1820's when the elder Pugin and Rickman each went to the continent and came back with drawings of French Gothic, occasional architects had followed in their footsteps, but there had never been such a widespread or concentrated study of French Gothic until the competitors for the Lille Cathedral went abroad to prepare themselves for the competition. Almost all of the designs showed the influence of their foreign studies. From then on the continental styles were used more freely by the Revivalists. Naturally there was a certain reaction against the introduction of Flemish, German and French styles, for it had long been held that the Gothic was the purely Eng-

[26] Verses 2 and 13 from "Mr. Molony's Account of the Crystal Palace," *Punch*, XX:171, April, 1851.

lish style of architecture. The stylistic nationalists fought a losing battle, for the mediaeval archaeologists were proving more and more incontrovertibly that the Gothic was not an indigenously English style, but originally a French style. The Lille competition to a great measure broke down the insularity of the English Gothic Revival, and led to the appreciation of the continental styles of Gothic building, which in turn led to the eclecticism of Victorian Gothic.

But even more responsible for the coming eclecticism were the writings of John Ruskin, especially the *Seven Lamps of Architecture* (1849) and the *Stones of Venice* (1851–53). Through his influence the most incongruous of mediaeval styles was introduced into England, namely, the Italian. This made the "steaky bacon" style of building which is the most repellant of all Victorian Gothics.

Ruskin has been generally called the most important figure in the Gothic Revival, and until recently there was a prevalent notion that he, through his analysis of the Gothic, had made the Revival possible. But now that we have more perspective with which to judge him and the movement, we still realize his importance, but give it a different emphasis.

John Ruskin lived from 1819 to 1900. He was the son of a wealthy wine merchant and a puritanical mother. They both early regarded their son as a genius, and for the fifty-two years that he lived with them, they tried to shield him from all unpleasant aspects of the world. He had a rigid religious training, but was never sent to a public school because of his delicate health. He early acquired a great enthusiasm for Turner and his first work, *Modern Painters*, was an attempt to point out his excellence. Until 1850 and the publication of the books already mentioned, he had had no connection with the Gothic Revival. In 1851 he came in contact with the Pre-Raphaelite Brotherhood which had been formed by Rossetti, Millais and Hunt. In 1855 he took an active interest in the building of the new Museum in Oxford. By 1860 his relations with the Gothic Revival had ceased. He became interested in Socialism and Maurice's workingmen's art classes and tried teaching in them for several years. His humanitarian leanings became stronger. His later books were concerned with the improvement of society and economics. His ideal was the mediaeval manorial system and in 1875 he tried the social experiment of founding the Guild of St. George, which was not successful and incurred only debts. During the last years of his life he was afflicted by recurring fits of insanity. But before his death he had given the English people a new consciousness of Art and Beauty.

The Seven Lamps of Architecture of which Ruskin writes are the Lamps of Sacrifice, Truth, Power, Beauty, Life, Memory and Obedience. Just to name them is sufficient to show how far he had travelled from the classical canons of Vitruvius and the ideas which guided the first English writer on architecture, Sir Henry Wotton, who wrote: "Well-building hath three conditions: Commodity, Firmness, and Delight." Ruskin's lamps are spiritual and moral, as is perhaps natural, as he was never a practicing architect. That was one reason that his writings had such an appeal: they were unencumbered by technical knowledge. The Lamps of Sacrifice and Life both have to do with the builders. The first emphasizes the spirit in which a great building should be undertaken and the latter the moral qualities. The Lamp of Truth is that of good construction, in which he is reminiscent of Pugin's *True Principles*. The Lamp of Beauty defines beauty as nature; and that in art which is beautiful as that which most closely follows nature. In the Lamp of Obedience, he concludes by saying that there can be no great style in England, "unless we are contented to submit architecture and all art, like other things, to English law." [26] He also tried to decide which style would be the most fitting for English architecture. "The choice would lie I think between four styles:— 1. The Pisan Romanesque; 2. The early Gothic of the western Italian Republics, advanced as far and as fast as our art would enable us to the Gothic of Giotto; 3. The Venetian Gothic in its purest development; 4. The English earliest decorated. The most natural, perhaps the safest choice, would be the last, well fenced from the chance of again stiffening into the perpendicular; and perhaps enriched by some mingling of decorative elements from the exquisite decorated Gothic of France." [27]

Ruskin always had a great dislike of English perpendicular, which was the style which the early Revivalists had used the most successfully. Notable examples of the use of this style were Fonthill Abbey, St. Luke's, Chelsea and the Parliament Buildings. It was generally admired, but not by Ruskin. "What a host of ugly church towers we have in England, with pinnacles at the corners, and none in the middle! How many buildings like King's College Chapel at Cambridge, looking like tables upside down, with their four legs in the air!" [28] One great reason that Ruskin did not like English mediaeval architecture was that he did not know it, while he studied stone by stone the buildings in Venice and made drawings of the cathedrals in France and

[26] Ruskin, *Seven Lamps*, p. 169.
[27] Ruskin, *Stones of Venice*, II:258.
[28] Ruskin, *Seven Lamps*, p. 164.

Italy. If Ruskin had had a robuster constitution, England might have been spared the wave of Venetian Gothic. The last paragraph of the preface to the first edition of the *Lamps* reads as follows: "I could have wished to have given more examples from our early English Gothic; but I have always found it impossible to work in the cold interiors of our cathedrals, while the daily services, lamps, and fumigation of those upon the Continent, render them perfectly safe. In the course of last summer I undertook a pilgrimage to the English Shrines, and began with Salisbury, where the consequence of a few days' work was a state of weakened health, which I may be permitted to name among the causes of the slightness and imperfection of the present Essay."

Ruskin was the great popularizer of the Gothic and that is why he has been given such a prominent place in the Gothic Revival. By the middle of the last century the reading public had increased enormously, so many read *The Stones of Venice* and learnt of the nature of the Gothic from Ruskin. Chapter six in volume two has the title "The Nature of the Gothic." It was immediately republished as a separate pamphlet and sold for sixpence to working men so that they might also know the nature of the Gothic. Therefore Ruskin's ideas rather than those of the architects became widely known.

He made an analysis of the Gothic style and came to the following conclusion. "I believe, then, that the characteristic or moral elements of Gothic are the following, placed in order of their importance:

1. Savageness   4. Grotesqueness
2. Changefulness   5. Rigidity
3. Naturalism   6. Redundance

These characters are here expressed as belonging to the building; as belonging to the builder, they would be expressed thus: 1. Savageness, or Rudeness. 2. Love of Change. 3. Love of Nature. 4. Disturbed Imagination. 5. Obstinacy. 6. Generosity. And I repeat, that the withdrawal of any one, or any two, will not at once destroy the Gothic character of a building, but the removal of a majority of them will." [29]

Architecture is a difficult art for the layman to enjoy, for in its purity it is abstract, like mathematics, and is completely without personal qualities. Ruskin, because he was not an architect and had an undisciplined and emotional mind, ignored the true principles of architecture and in all sincerity substituted moral and spiritual qualities. These were easily understood by his readers, and they were as willing to see savageness in Gothic architecture as the previous century had been to see the picturesque.

Ruskin's early religious training had been rigidly Protestant, and he tried to remain true to it all his life. By nature he was sensuous, and the color, motion and incense of the Roman Catholic Church immediately appealed to him. He felt compelled to fight against this tendency and his one great achievement was to divorce Gothic from Roman Catholic ritual, by emphasizing the non-religious characteristics which are quoted above.

In this century there has been a strong reaction against Ruskinism, but in his own day he was universally held to be the Apostle of Aesthetic Enlightenment. He was Slade Professor of Art at Oxford and exerted great influence on the undergraduates. He was a popular lecturer and gave many talks before all types of organizations, even the Royal

[29] Ruskin, *Stones of Venice*, II: 184.

Institute of British Architects. The greatest change in art history which is due to his enthusiasms is the stress now laid on early Italian art, the Primitives and the Byzantine mosaics.

He has been held responsible for the moral attitude toward art which was prevalent during the end of Victoria's reign, and it is true that he always looked for the moral qualities not only of a work of art, but also of the artist. He could not appreciate the "Majestas" in Siena because Duccio had been in prison. He was prone to judge the goodness of art by the goodness of the artist. But this was not his own invention; the Cambridge Camden Society for ten years before had been stressing the need for individual goodness as an integral part of good architecture, and publishing pamphlets exhorting masons to live good and holy lives and bricklayers to refrain from swearing. The close interdependence of morality and art which was a characteristic of the Victorian aesthetics was, perhaps, merely the unconscious diffusion of the preachings of Wesley and part of the reaction against the skepticism of the previous century.

Ruskin's interpretation of beauty was important, for it broke down the last vestiges of classic prestige, by proving that Greek geometrical ornament was ugly because it was not like nature. Ruskinism, as this system of aesthetics is generally called, defined Beauty as Nature or that which is most like to natural forms. It is pernicious because Nature is impossible to imitate, or to recreate. It imposes God-made standards instead of human ones, and no artist can live up to them.

Gibbon, the historian, went to Venice and found it a dirty, unattractive place, one of the least pleasing in Europe. Joseph Woods when he was in Venice about 1825 wrote that he found nothing worth looking at there. Ruskin went in the forties and found it beautiful. He was responsible for the vogue for Venice and north Italy which animated the aesthetes of the end of the century. But whether Ruskin can be held accountable for the eclecticism of Victorian Gothic is another question. It was probably bound to come and the enthusiasm of Ruskin merely intensified and hastened it. He sanctioned it and encouraged it, although he several times tried to point out that early English Decorated Gothic was the most sensible choice for English architects. At all events, the late Gothic Revival was different from the early and Ruskin clearly enunciated the tenets which changed it.

In the third quarter of the nineteenth century there were many architects who could be discussed as Gothic Revivalists. The most important was Gilbert Scott. There are at least four others who must be mentioned. Butterfield, whose most known work is All Saints Church in Margaret Street, London, combined an interest in the Gothic with a preoccupation in logical construction. Philip Webb carried on the traditions of Pugin and remained aloof from the new tendencies introduced by Ruskin. Waterhouse was held in high favor by the Revivalists, for his plans for the new Assize Courts and the Town Hall, Manchester, were accepted in 1859. They were Gothic sprinkled with Italian ornament. Ruskin considered them "much beyond everything yet done in England on my principles." And lastly, Street, who published in 1855 a book entitled, *Brick and Marble in the Middle Ages,* which served as a reference book for those who wished to put in practice the newly admired Italian Gothic. Street's greatest triumph was to win the competition for the New Law Courts. The revivalists considered that this was the end of the Battle of the Styles in 1868 and that the Goths had won, but by the time that the Law Courts were finished in 1884, the Gothic Revival as a dominant style in English architecture existed no longer and eclecticism reigned undisputed.

The reason for this change was that the two most brilliant of the youngest generation of Gothic Revivalists introduced a new architectural modification which was known by the name of the Queen Anne Style. It was inspired by the early eighteenth century which still showed the influence of the Dutch styles which had been introduced during the reign of William and Mary. It has also been called a Modified-Renaissance style, which soon became even more similar to the Italian Renaissance styles of the fifteenth century. The two architects were Eden Nesfield and R. Norman Shaw. The first important building of the Queen Anne style, which succeeded the Gothic Revival, was designed by the latter in 1873, namely the New Zealand Chambers in London.

This of course does not mean that modern buildings were no longer built in the Gothic styles. The most basic reason for ending the Gothic Revival in 1870 is that by then, the great majority of churches had been built and there was more civic and domestic architecture from then on. Also, that the Revivalists had done their work. Every architect working in the Gothic manner tried to be archaeologically correct. The principles of Gothic construction were generally known, especially after the publication of Viollet-le-Duc's *Dictionary*. Every church architect conformed to the ground plans as set forth by the *Ecclesiologist*. The nineteenth century had no one style of building, but during the middle of the century there were architects who worked almost exclusively in the Gothic mode.

The Gothic styles were used after 1870 and are still used today, but generally for ecclesiastical or collegiate buildings. There have been many edifices built in the Gothic Revival style since 1870, but two merit particular mention. The first is the new cathedral at Truro designed by J. L. Pearson in the Early English style and built between 1880 and 1910. It is an impressive and imposing building which is faithful in all details to mediaeval architecture. The interior is particularly pleasing. By some architectural critics, it is considered to be the last and the best of the churches built by the Gothic Revivalists and to be the culmination of the imitative Gothic of the nineteenth century. These writers feel that a new era of Gothic building came in with the new century, that is one of free adaptation of the mediaeval styles based upon a more profound understanding of the structural principles of the Middle Ages which was possible only after the publication of Viollet-le-Duc's *Dictionary*. They consider that the cathedral at Liverpool is the best expression of this new use of the Gothic style. The cathedral is not yet finished but when it is it will be the largest cathedral in England with a total length of 482 feet and a total area of 101,000 square feet. It was designed by Giles Gilbert Scott, the grandson of the great Scott, at the age of twenty-one, but the original plan has since been modified. The building was begun in 1904. The only parts which are finished are the Choir, East Transepts and the Lady Chapel, which was consecrated in 1910. This cathedral is sufficient to show that the style brought into vogue by the Gothic Revival is still, although somewhat modified, in existence.

In writing the history of an architectural style, it is too easy to become engrossed in it and omit references to general history. It gives the impression that architecture was produced in a vacuum, which is unfortunate, but easily understandable. An architectural style, once that it is accepted, continues with little influence on or from current events. So it is with the Gothic Revival in England. The style began with the vogue for Gothic ornament. It spread with the vogue for literature which dealt with the Middle Ages. It became firmly planted with the revival of the Anglican Church in the 1830's and '40's. By 1850, it was established. The character of the revival changed from a national one to a cosmopolitan one owing to the travels and studies of the architects and the writings of Ruskin.

The style spread to many countries with the diffusion of English culture and imperialism. Therefore, in Canada, the Parliament Buildings at Ottawa are mediaeval in style. In Australia there is modern Gothic. In India, the railway station at Bombay and the Great Clock Tower in Delhi are modern Gothic. The history of the British Empire explains the diffusion of Victorian Gothic.

Most people are little conscious of buildings, so it seems unwarranted to read too much into the influence of architecture on society, although architecture is generally conceded to be the expression of society. In this case the Gothic Revival is an expression of the romanticism, national pride and religious feeling of English society in the nineteenth century.

Chapter IV

GOTHIC IN MODERN FRANCE

In France, during the Middle Ages, a great number of cathedrals, abbeys and monasteries were built, but they have not always been admired. In the early years of the sixteenth century the fashion for the Italian Renaissance was introduced into France under the enthusiastic leadership of Francis I. The vogue for the classic traditions in art prospered throughout the century and became universal in the seventeenth century. French mediaevalists who are eager to show that the taste for Gothic architecture never completely died out in France cite, to prove the continuance of the tradition, the construction of St. Gervais, St. Etienne du Mont and St. Eustache in the 1500's. The ground plans and basic construction of these churches are Gothic, but the detail and the ornament is unmistakably Renaissance. During the seventeenth and eighteenth centuries practically no Gothic buildings were erected in France, because Gothic was not good taste.

In the Battle of the Ancients and the Moderns, which took place about 1680, Perrault and Fontenelle were as convinced as La Fontaine that the Dark Ages had contributed almost nothing to human progress and knowledge. All the great writers of the Age of Louis XIV were united in ignoring the Middle Ages; Molière and Fénelon as well as Corneille and Racine.

This is of course not surprising for the Middle Ages had not yet come into their own. Voetius and Cellarius were just beginning to distinguish history into three main periods and to write of the Church in the Middle Ages, but to most people the Dark Ages were still very dark indeed. In France, the Benedictines, especially those of the Congregation of St. Maur, were the first to make an historical study of the mediaeval period and to gather documents to further the study. I suspect that the motivating factor of the Benedictines was a latent antagonism to the Jesuits who were very important at this time, but a comparatively new order, founded in 1540. The Jesuits were the great spokesmen of the reformed, post-Council of Trent Roman Catholic Church. The Benedictines were greatly criticized by the new order, but they had a long and glorious history which went back to the sixth century, so perhaps partly in self-defense they retired into their monasteries and delved into the past. The most famous of the Maurists was Jean Mabillon whose *De Re Diplomatica,* published in 1681, is still used as a basis for dating mediaeval documents and detecting forgeries. His treatise on monastic orders published ten years later in another keystone in mediaeval history.

The interest in mediaeval history which the Benedictine scholars first displayed in the seventeenth century has continued until the present. A great deal of work was done in the eighteenth century. Dom Bernard de Montfaucon was one of the most active and after 1750 published a great deal on the Middle Ages. This scholarship, however, did not affect the generality of the French. The general tendency was in the other direction, for the majority of the French writers were very critical of the Church and had a wholesome scorn for the past and a great enthusiasm for the future.

Eighteenth-century France was not happy economically. It was suffering under the great debts incurred by Louis XIV and John Law's even more disastrous attempt to recoup the fortunes of France. Socially, it was equally unhappy, for the middle class was heavily taxed and yet had no social position. There was general dissatisfaction. This was aggravated by the Anglomania which was prevalent in the second quarter of the century. Voltaire spent three years in England (1726–29) and his *Lettres Anglaises* published in 1734 had a great deal to do with spreading the vogue. But before he went to England there had been three large and important publications which show that he was but one of many interested in English customs and literature. Between 1717 and 1728 appeared the *Bibliothéque Anglaise;* between 1720 and 1724 came out *Mémoires littéraires de la Grande-Bretagne,* and at the same time the monumental, twenty-five volume work edited by Prévost and Demazeau, the *Bibliothéque Britannique.* This wave of Anglomania culminated in *L'Esprit des Lois* by Montesquieu which was published in 1748.

Naturally this interest in English customs was not confined to politics and government, but manners and dress were also affected. One phase of this interest in England touches our subject, that is landscape gardening. Early in the eighteenth century the English became tired of formal gardens, and picturesque gardens were designed instead. These simulated nature, with vistas, artificial wildness and ruins. French visitors were charmed by these and a few had their gardens remodelled on picturesque principles. Two of the most famous parks *à l'anglais* were Ermonville and that planned by Kléber for the Prince of Montbéliard in Alsace in 1787. Various other parks had Gothic ruins and this coming fashion has the name of the troubadour style. It seems to have been more ephemeral and less important than the contemporary Strawberry Hill Gothic in England.

There are several instances of a more serious concern in Gothic architecture.[1a] As early as 1708 a paper was given in the Academy of Architects which praised mediaeval architecture. In 1761 the French Academy discussed the technique of Gothic vaulting in connection with the proposed restoration and completion of the cathedral at Strasbourg. Some restoration was done. The Abbey Church of Poissy was restored about 1726 (destroyed 1802), and the Cathedral at Orleans where J. J. Gabriel tried to design in the Gothic style, but his attempts were less pleasing than those of Sir Christopher Wren.

Under the Ancien Régime there are a few evidences of the coming vogue for the Moyen Age which is so widespread after the Restoration of Louis XVIII. But the coming interest is not easily discernible for several reasons. The most important is that art in France was dominated by the court which was not intrigued by the Gothic, but produced strong, original styles: *l'art classique* under Louis XIV, the Rococo under Louis XV, and the Greek revival under Louis XVI. Their desire for novelty was pacified by the Chinoiseries. Almost every town house and château had a room decorated with scenes of Chinese about the middle of the century. The Chinese Chippendale and the English Canton made at Lowestoft show that the English were also pleased

[1a] Lawson, *Le Gôut de moyen âge en France au XVIIIe siécle* gives the best account of the subject.

by the Orient, but theirs was but a passing fancy in comparison to the French vogue.

It was very natural that the cultivated Frenchman should be pleased to have a Chinoiserie rather than a Gothic summerhouse, for the myth of the Chinese sage was in favor, while the mediaeval monk and the Church were definitely out of favor. The writers were all beginning to discuss the natural goodness of man, an idea which they got from Locke and changed to suit their purposes. But man was no longer good in France and the two powers which had perverted this natural goodness were the Monarchy and the Church. So naturally they disliked everything which had to do with the past of these two institutions. Voltaire called Gothic architecture a fantastic compound of rudeness and filigree. The Middle Ages were not yet greatly admired.

A few historical subjects were painted after 1755 when d'Angiviller gave the artists of the Academy a list of subjects capable of arousing patriotism, which might lead the unwary into thinking that there was a real interest in the Middle Ages. They must be noted; but the paintings are definitely eighteenth-century, no matter at what period the event depicted took place.

The French Revolution used to be held responsible for all the damage done to mediaeval buildings before the time of Viollet-le-Duc. At present there is a reaction and the revolutionaries are found to be responsible for but a small fraction of the destruction of mediaeval art. During the seventeenth and eighteenth centuries the Gothic buildings were permitted to fall into disrepair. The chanons, in a passion for classic art, tore down the *jubés* which separated the choir from the nave. For years stones were taken from the old buildings to be used in new edifices. Some damage was done of course because the Revolution was anti-Catholic, but the greater damage wrought by neglect had been done before.

French historians of mediaeval art take more and more pride in pointing out that the first museum including the art of the Middle Ages was opened in 1791 by Lenoir in the convent of the Petits-Augustins. This Musée des monuments français played an important role in forming the taste of the nineteenth-century mediaevalists. Lenoir gathered fragments from Notre-Dame and from St. Denis and placed together examples of the different periods of Romanesque and Gothic art. He published an excellent catalogue of the collection. He may have been more actuated by patriotic motives than by aesthetic ones, but still he made accessible examples of French mediaeval art and gave them an importance which had not been accorded them before.

The style of the Empire was classical with Egyptian variations. How very classical the taste was is best proved by remembering the decorations for the coronation of Napoleon at Notre-Dame in Paris. A classic façade was painted and put up and the interior was transformed as much as possible into a classic edifice. La Madeleine is the best known building which testifies to the pervading classicism. It is true, nevertheless, that Napoleon was fond of Ossian and had murals depicting scenes from the poems painted at Malmaison.

Two books were published during the Napoleonic period which had such influence on men's minds that, with the Restoration, a flood of mediaevalism spread over the land. The first and most important book was *Le Génie du Christianisme* by Chateaubriand, which came out in five volumes

in 1802. It was a magnificent panegyric of the Roman
Catholic Church and even more of the fundamental principles of Christianity. It compared Milton with Homer to
find the latter lacking, and the former rich in all good qualities. It described, yet wrapt in mystery, the sacraments of
the Church. It told of the many good deeds which the
Church had performed. It pointed out the shamefulness of
the neglect accorded the abbeys and churches, which had
formerly been the scene of such respect and power among
the people. It derided Voltaire and deplored his pernicious
influence on the faith of the people. It attempted to prove
the beauty and inspiration of Christianity, and offered as
evidence the Gothic Cathedrals and Chivalry. "On ne pou-
vait entrer dans une église gothique sans éprouver une
sorte de frissonnement et un sentiment vague de la Divi-
nité." [1]

In the last chapter, Chateaubriand concludes that "le
christianisme a sauvé la société d'une destruction totale." [2]
And he presents the syllogism that Christianity is perfect;
man is imperfect, and yet he knows of it: "Donc le christianisme est une religion révélée." [3] With which sentence, he
brings the book to an end.

It is a lyric and moving work, written with evident sincerity by an ardent believer. It gave courage and strength
to the conservatives and the faithful. A reaction against
the skepticism and atheism of the eighteenth century was
bound to come. This book focused it and united it with the
Catholic Church. It was one of the most read books of the
century and took the place in France of the Tractarians,

[1] Chateaubriand, *Le Génie du Christianisme*, Pt. 3, bk. 2, chap. 8,
p. 366.
[2] *Ibid.*, Pt. 4, bk. 6, chap. 13, p. 272.   [3] *Ibid.*, p. 280.

the High Church Movement and Methodism in England. There was no religious revival in France comparable to the one in England, but *Le Génie* did bring a number of wandering souls back to the flock and counteracted the influence of the Age of Reason. And naturally as people came back to the Church they also began to take an interest in the history of the Church and the architecture of the cathedrals and soon there was a growing appreciation of the Gothic.

The importance of Chateaubriand in forming the Romantic School in France is well summarized by Gautier. "Chateaubriand peut être consideré comme l'aïeul ou, si vous l'aimez mieux, comme le Sachem du Romantisme en France. Dans le *Génie du Christianisme,* il restaura la cathédrale gothique; dans les *Natchez,* il rouvrit la grande nature fermée; dans *René,* il inventa la mélancolie et la passion moderne." [4]

The other book which did so much to make the French conscious of the Middle Ages was *De l'Allemagne* by Madame de Staël. She was exiled by Napoleon and spent her time travelling. She went to Germany and Austria, where she became acquainted with the German Romanticists and especially A. W. Schlegel, who became her good friend and travelling companion.

By 1804, the German scholars had been talking and writing of Gothic and romantic for several years. As Madame de Staël said, "The word romantic has been recently introduced into Germany to describe the poetry inspired by the songs of the troubadours, chivalry and Christianity." [5] A patriotic awakening had gripped Germany and even phi-

---

[4] Gautier, *Histoire du Romantisme,* p. 4.
[5] de Staël, *De l'Allemagne,* II:10.

losophers were becoming nationalistic. Schlegel's contribution was to emphasize the naturally romantic nature of German history and literature. Madame de Staël took this over and enlarged upon it. Her thesis was that there are two different temperaments in Europe: the southern one which expresses itself in classic forms, and the northern, in romantic. "Si l'on n'admet pas que le paganisme et le Christianisme, le Nord et le Midi, l'antiquité et le moyen âge, le chevalerie et les institutions grecques et romaines, se sont partagé l'empire de la littérature, l'on ne pas viendra jamais à juger sous un point de vue philosophique le goût antique et le goût moderne." [6]

The work was published in 1810, but immediately confiscated by the order of Napoleon, and was not republished until three years later in London. It was not widely read until the downfall of Napoleon, when the authoress returned to France. She died soon after, in 1817, but the ideas which she had culled during her exile became more and more popular. She did not appreciate the classicism of French literature and felt that it should be romantic to be in keeping with the spirit and history of the country. "Le littérature des anciens est chez les modernes une littérature transplantée: la littérature romantique ou chevaleresque est chez nous indigène, et c'est notre religion et nos institutions qui l'ont fait éclore." [7] "La littérature romantique est la seule qui sont susceptible encore d'être perfectionnée, parce qu'ayant ses racines dans notre propre sol, elle est la seule qui puisse croître et se vivifier de nouveau; elle exprime notre religion; elle rapelle notre histoire; son origine est ancienne, mais non antique." [8]

The younger generation which Gautier described so well

[6] *Ibid.*, p. 12.   [7] *Ibid.*, p. 15.   [8] *Ibid.*, p. 17.

took up the notion with particular fervor and looked into the past history of France, into the mediaeval buildings, and into their own souls to find the romantic. They wanted to break with the cold formalism of *l'art classique de Louis XIV*, and to find freedom and self-expression through the age of chivalry, to be troubadours of the nineteenth century. Madame de Staël, in large measure, by stating that the north was romantic, made France romantic. And her assertion, gleaned from the Germans, that the best source of romanticism was the Middle Ages, began an intense interest in the shadowy past, and with it an appreciation of the standing memorials of that time, the Gothic cathedrals.

The cult of the mediaeval started in France after the Restoration. It is important to note that the works of Sir Walter Scott were first translated into French and published in 1816. He was almost as popular in France as in England, and certainly the Waverley Novels played their part in making society *moyenâgeuse*. His influence is discernible, also, in the literature of the period, especially in the works of Hugo and Dumas.[9]

Théophile Gautier was a young man in 1830 and one of *les vrais romantiques*. In his old age in 1868, long after the fireworks of the Romantic Movement had burnt out, he looked back at this period with nostalgia and wrote, "Quel temps merveilleux! Walter Scott était alors dans toute sa fleur de succès; on s'initiait aux mystères du *Faust* de Goethe, qui contient tout, selon l'expression de madame de Staël, et même quelque chose d'un peu plus que tout. On découvrait Shakespeare sous la traduction un peu raccommodée de Letourneur, et les poëmes de lord Byron, *le Cor-*

---

[9] See Louis Maigron, *Le Roman Historique à l'Epoque Romantique*.

saire, Lara, le Giaour, Manfred, Beppo, Don Juan, nous arrivaient de l'Orient, qui n'etait pas banal encore. Comme tout cela était jeune, nouveau, étrangement coloré, d'enivrante et forte saveur! La tête nous en tournait; il semblait qu'on entrait dans des mondes inconnus." [10]

The French architects remained on the whole aloof from the vagaries of the Romantic Movement. Nevertheless, directly after the Restoration, one royal chapel was built which used the mediaeval instead of the classic style. That was the Chapelle l'Orleans at Dreux which was begun by Percier in 1816 and finished by Lefranc in 1847.

In 1821 the decorations for the baptism of the duc de Bordeaux showed the growing taste for the mediaeval. Even more noteworthy were decorations for the coronation of Charles X in 1825. Charles was the first monarch to show a definite interest in Gothic art, and we are indebted to him for the purchase of the Durand collection and also of the Revoil collection which form the most noteworthy part of the collection in the Louvre of mediaeval minor arts.

Popular taste was being weaned from the classic and taught to appreciate the mediaeval by the publication of volumes of illustrations, which were similar to those of Grose and Carter which had appeared in England and the contemporary volumes of Britton. Millin, Seroux d'Agincourt, d'Aumont and Chapuy all published works about 1823. The series of French cathedrals, published between 1816–36 by Alexander de Laborde; and *Voyages pittoresques et romantiques dans l'ancienne France* begun by Baron Taylor in 1820 and continued by Nodier and Cailleux until 1864, are the most important.

The patriotic sentiments aroused by the Revolution and

[10] Gautier, *op. cit.,* p. 5.

the conquests of Napoleon led to an increasing preoccupation on the part of the historians in the Middle Ages.
Michaud's *Histoire des Croisades* which came out in 1808
is one of the earliest, but it was followed by Thierry's
Lettres sur l'histoire de France and Michelet's *Histoire de
France* and later in 1823 by Guizot's *Collection des
Mémories relatif à l'histoire de France*. These are but
samples. But all these works were written with a definitely
partisan bias. The French historians were determined to
prove that they had the most glorious history, and were
really the only civilized people in the Middle Ages. Guizot's
Histoire de la Civilization distinctly gives that impression
as he apologizes for the vastness of his subject, and then
says that he will be concerned mostly with the history of
France since so much began or was perfected there. The
historians laid the ground work for the nationalistic bias
which characterizes French archaeology.

A genuine interest in the past led to the formation of innumerable societies. In 1814 the Société Nationale des
Antiquaires de France was started. Provincial societies
soon were formed in each province; the first of these was
started by Arcisse de Caumont in Normandy in 1823. Caumont played a significant role, for he was the first professor
of mediaeval archaeology in France at the University of
Caen and made the subject possible by his own researches.
In 1833 the Congrés Scientifiques de France were started
which have yearly contributed so much to the general
knowledge of mediaeval buildings in France. The next year
was formed the Société Français d'Archéologie pour la conservation des Monuments Historiques. Also was started
the *Bulletin Monumental* under the leadership of Palustre,
Marsy and the great Lefèvre-Pontalis. On the tenth of

January, 1835, Guizot formed the Comité des Documents Inédits. These societies made a careful study of the monuments which were about them and gathered together a great deal of information. They were primarily concerned with learning the constructional principles and the origins, which they believed to be found in the Ile de France and so heightened their patriotic interest in the Gothic architecture.

The July Revolution of 1830 brought to power the historians and men of letters. They had been touched by the new movements of romanticism and mediaevalism before taking office, and after they became officials or allied to the government their whims and fancies became the fashion. The Bourgeois king himself entered into the spirit of the decade and commissioned murals for a Hall of Crusades at Versailles.

The liberals who were also mediaevalists tried to connect their enthusiasms. Vitet, for example, said, "the principle of Gothic architecture is in freedom, liberty, in the spirit of association and camaraderie, in feelings which are completely native to us and national." It may seem difficult to us to reconcile political liberalism and Gothic architecture, but the Men of Thirty were determined to see liberalism everywhere. Hugo in the preface to *Hernani* defined romanticism as the spirit of liberalism in literature. "Le romantisme, tant de fois mal défini, n'est à tout prendre, . . . que le liberalisme en litterature." [11]

The work which best brought back the Middle Ages and made them popular in France was *Notre-Dame de Paris* by Victor Hugo. The influence of Walter Scott is clearly discernible in it, but that does not lessen its value. It is a

[11] Hugo, preface to *Hernani*, p. 1.

story of Paris during the reign of Louis XI and the cathedral of Notre-Dame plays a dominating role. It is generally
said that the publication of this book in 1831 was in large
measure responsible for the restoration of the cathedral
begun in 1843. The book has been called an ode to the
cathedral and the following sentence, which describes the
façade, is in itself sufficient to make the criticism valid.
". . . il est, à coup sûr, peu de plus belles pages architec-
turales que cette façade où, successivement et à la fois, les
trois portails creusée en ogive, le cordon brodé et dentelé
des vingt-huit niches royales, l'immense rosace centrale
flanquée de ses deux fenêtres latérales comme le prêtre du
diacre et du sous-diacre, la haute et frêle galerie d'arcades
à trèfle qui porte une lourde plate-forme sur ses fines colon-
nettes, enfin les deux noires et massives tours avec leurs
auvents d'ardoise, parties harmonieuses d'un tout magni-
fique, superposées en cinq étages gigantesques, se dévelop-
pent a l'œil, en foule et sans touble, avec leurs innomerables
de statuaire, de sculpture et de ciselure, ralliés puissam-
ment à la tranquille grandeur de l'ensemble; vaste sym-
phonie en pierre, pour ainsi dire; œuvre colossale d'un
homme et d'un peuple, tout ensemble une et complexe
comme les Iliades et les romanceros dont elle est sœur;
produit prodigieux de la cotisation de toutes les forces d'une
époque, où sur chaque pierre on voit saillir en cent façons
la fantasie de l'ouvrier disciplinée par le génie de l'artiste;
sorte de création humaine, en un mot, puissante et féconde
comme la création divine dont elle semble avoir dérobé le
double caractère: variété, éternité." [12]

This fashion for mediaevalism touched all aspects of
society. Young men wore their hair long à la Charlemagne.

[12] Hugo, *Notre Dame,* Bk. 3, chap. 1, p. 164.

They grew beards à la Barbarossa. The ladies wore head-dresses à la St. Louis or à la Clodion le Chevelu. Cloaks and flowing robes became fashionable. Jewelers made brooches and lockets in the mediaeval style. Furniture was designed after Gothic models. The Salons were full of historical paintings representing mediaeval scenes. Balls were given to which all the guests had to come as mediaeval characters. It became fashionable to have a room done over in a Gothic style, as a Chinoiserie had been in vogue in the preceding century. Plays, operas and novels were inspired by the Middle Ages. Society was moyenâgeuse.[13]

Despite this fad comparatively few houses were built or remodeled in Gothic styles. The chef de cabinet aux Beaux-Arts, A. de Beauchesne, had a Gothic manor built near the château Madrid in the Bois de Boulogne. The château de la Reine Blanche at Chantilly, designed by Fontaine in 1826, was one of the earliest. In Paris in the Place de Caire there was a Maison Egyptienne which had one story in a Gothic style. The Maison des Gothes, at 116 rue St. Martin, with a Flamboyant façade, was one of the most famous. One of the latest built about 1850 was the house of Viollet-le-Duc in the rue Calliot.

Not many churches were designed either, because there was no need for new churches in France. The Jesuits had sprinkled the country with new churches in the seventeenth century and neither the population nor the religious enthusiasm had grown sufficiently to need any more. A certain number were built. In Paris there were two which should be mentioned, although they had little architectural value. One was the church in Montmartre designed in 1835

[13] Maigron, *Le Romantisme et la Mode* gives an excellent and detailed account of this vogue.

by the Comte de l'Escalofier, which was destroyed in 1882. The other, the "romanesquoid" church, of St. Ferdinand, designed by Fontaine.

There is in Paris only one church which was built in the nineteenth century which can compare with the Gothic Revival churches in England. It is Ste. Clotilde on the Left Bank. It was very appropriate to dedicate the new church to a Merovingian saint who was connected with the early history of Paris. It is built of white stone and lavishly decorated. It is fourteenth-century in style and has two spires on the façade which are perforated like those at Burgos, Strasbourg or Cologne. The details are mediaeval in character and the ground plan is typical. In the construction there was an innovation which interested the contemporary architects and in 1857 a description of the church appeared. The innovation was the use of cast iron ribs in the roof, which insured firm vaulting. The iron girders were masked by the stone blocks of the vaults, and so were invisible, but were of great value in the construction.

This church was designed by François Christian Gau in 1846. It was finished after his death by Theodore Ballu. Gau was born in 1790 in Cologne. He studied in Italy and was naturalized a Frenchman in 1821. He became an important French architect filling many commissions until his death in 1850. He was made architect of the Bank of France and la Ville de Paris. He restored St. Julien-le-Pauvre and designed a new presbytery for St. Severin. His publications with Niebuhr on the Nile and with Mazois on Pompeii are known to students. But his greatest claim to fame is Ste. Clotilde, which is one of the best examples of an original design done in a Gothic style in France.

The Competition for the Lille Cathedral in 1855 was won by the Englishmen, Burges, first prize, and Street, second prize. That suggests that the jury found the English architects the most skillful in Gothic designs. The great reason that so few French architects devoted their talents to Gothic designs was the attitude of the Ecole des Beaux-Arts, which school held a semi-official and almost despotic position. The school has always been conservative, and to succeed as an architect in France it is almost necessary to be affiliated with the Ecole des Beaux-Arts.

If there was not much original work in the Gothic tradition done in France during the nineteenth century, nevertheless, great attention was paid to the Gothic buildings which remained from the Middle Ages. Guizot, the minister under Louis Philippe and the historian of the Middle Ages, formed in 1837 the Commission pour la Conservation des Monuments Historiques. Vitet was first made Commissioner and later Prosper Mérimée. Their function was to make a survey of the mediaeval monuments which needed restoration, to appoint an architect and to supervise the work. The first church which they decided needed repair was the abbey church at Vézelay and the architect they chose was Viollet-le-Duc, although he was not yet thirty years old. He was successful, and so began his life work.

Eugène Emmanuel Viollet-le-Duc was born in 1813 and died in 1879. He had the usual Beaux-Arts training, then travelled across France with Delécluze and Mérimée, and went to Italy where he preferred Bramante to Palladio and was particularly pleased with the Villa Medici. His friend Mérimée was responsible for his first commission in 1840, the restoration at Vézelay. That was so satisfactory that many other commissions followed. He worked with Lassus on Ste. Chapelle and the cathedral of Notre-Dame in Paris. He also worked at Amiens, Chartres, Reims, Troyes, Clermont-Ferrand and many other places. On almost all the monuments of the Middle Ages which we admire today in France, there is to be seen the work of Viollet-le-Duc and nineteenth-century sculptors and masons. For example, at Notre-Dame at Paris, there is only one statue about the portals which is not nineteenth-century, and that is the Saint Anne on the trumeau of the north portal.

The Commission which supervised the restoration of ancient monuments in France was started under the July Monarchy, but the greater part of the work was done during the Second Empire, for Napoleon the Third took a great interest in the work. He may have in part inherited this enthusiasm from his mother, Queen Hortense, who was very moyenâgeuse and influenced by the Romantics. The two restorations of non-religious mediaeval architecture which he was particularly interested in and which were done by Viollet-le-Duc were the restorations of the citadel at Carcassonne and the château of Pierrefonds. Napoleon was so pleased by the work that he tried to make Viollet-le-Duc professor at the Ecole des Beaux-Arts. He did receive the appointment and gave the lectures for one year, but the conservative group was so powerful and so opposed to this official sanction of the Gothic, that the Emperor was forced to rescind the appointment and the Beaux-Arts remained the citadel of classicism.

The criticism which the Gothic received caused Viollet-le-Duc to write his monumental *Dictionary* which has molded our ideas of mediaeval architecture, even as his restorations have formed part of our visual impressions of it. Even as early as 1846 Lassus and Viollet-le-Duc began writing to defend themselves and the style in which they worked. In 1857 Lassus edited the *Album of Villard de Honnecourt* which is in the Bibliothéque Nationale. De Honnecourt was a thirteenth-century architect who made sketches of Reims, Laon, Amiens and other Gothic buildings. He also made designs and ground plans and his drawings show that he had an advanced knowledge of mathematics and geometric design. Viollet-le-Duc made great use of this Album to show the importance and skill of mediaeval architects.

Le Dictionnaire raisonné de l'architecture français du XIe au XVIe siècle appeared between 1854 and 1869. It was really a collection of essays. The most influential, and perhaps the most famous, was the one entitled "Construction." In this he emphasized the logical method of building used in the Middle Ages. He proved that Gothic architecture was organic, that is that every stone had a purpose and use, that all the decoration and ornament was part of the structure of the building, that there was nothing unnecessary or added merely for effect. Pugin had already said this in England, but no one had in France.

The *Dictionary*, however, not only increased the general understanding and appreciation of the Gothic but also, by its insistence on the importance of good building and logical construction and functional planning, led the way directly to the twentieth-century innovations in architecture.

Viollet-le-Duc is by far the most important French architect connected with the Gothic in Modern France. His restorations and his writings make him preëminent. He was too busy to do much original work;[14] perhaps he was fortunate for there was very little demand for new buildings

[14] None of the few buildings which he designed were Gothic.

in the Gothic tradition in France. In the last quarter of the century there were several churches built which are considered mediaeval but they are not Gothic, but more Byzantine and eastern in style. In Paris the best known are La Trinité, St. Augustin, the church at Montrouge and Sacre-Cœur. The last was designed by one of the best known of Viollet's pupils, Paul Abadie, and begun in 1871 and is not yet finished. Of the provincial churches, perhaps the best known is the cathedral of Notre-Dame la Major, at Marseilles, designed by Vaudoyer, which is definitely Islo-Byzantine with domes and alternating bands of colored marbles.

The new interest in the Middle Ages in France did not lead to much imitative work in architecture. Instead it led to extensive restoration of the existing monuments. Also it encouraged historians and archaeologists. Above all it intensified and strengthened patriotic and nationalistic sentiments.

CHAPTER V

MODERN GOTHIC IN GERMANY

VERY FEW modern Gothic buildings were erected in Germany before 1840; after which date for about fifty years a goodly number were built. The German architects were led to the new style through the interest in the completion of the cathedral at Cologne and the success of the Gothic Revival in England. But the influences which made this modern Gothic acceptable had been at work in Germany since about 1760.

One authority for dating so early the first interest in the Gothic and the mediaeval in Germany is the *Dichtung und Wahrheit* of Goethe. In that he relates that his grandfather Textor and many of the citizens of Frankfurt took a great interest in antiquities and the early history of the town.

By that time also the two schools of the Classicists under Gottsched and the Moderns with Haller, Bödmer and Breitinger, and most important, Klopstock, were clearly defined. In the next decade the poetry of the Moderns found a champion in Herder, by whom the literary principles of romanticism were first enunciated.

Herder (1744–1803) read with attention the works of Rousseau and accepted the prevalent idea that primitive peoples were good and gifted. Very soon after their publication, Herder read the ballads collected in Bishop Percy's *Reliques* and the heroic tales of Ossian, which he considered to be authentic of the third century and not contemporary.

117

This poetry he found to be very pleasing, much more so than the stilted verse which was being turned out in Berlin on the French classical models. This poetry was by primitive peoples. Ossian lived in an uncivilized society and yet he told of chivalrous and heroic deeds. Ossian fitted very well into the general conception of the Noble Savage which in a large measure explains his popularity. Herder then evolved the theory of poetic creation which connected primitive society with spontaneous poetic expression. To back this notion he became more and more interested in folk songs, ballads, epics and mediaeval romances.

At this time, 1770–71, Goethe was studying in Strassburg and Herder came there to have an operation on his eye. Goethe was five years younger than Herder and eager to make his acquaintance. He did, and was much influenced by Herder's enthusiasm for the Middle Ages. The product of their friendship was the publication in 1773 of *Von Deutscher Art und Kunst, einige fliegende Blätter,* a small anonymous book containing essays by Herder, Goethe and Möser which praised the liberty of the ancient Germans, the Volkslieder, Shakespeare, Ossian, the Strassburg cathedral and Gothic art in general.[1] The essay on the cathedral was written by Goethe and in his memoirs written in 1811, he tells how difficult it had been for him at first to see any beauty or design in this building which was so different from the classical buildings which he had admired. It was Herder who had encouraged him to this work and it is generally considered to be the first appreciation accorded a mediaeval building written in the German language. This

[1] The latter subject was treated in an essay translated from the Italian of the Theologian and Mathematician, Paolo Frisi, "An Inquiry into Gothic Architecture," written in 1766.

book was really the first pronouncement of the Romantic School and had an immediate effect upon German writers and led them to study Old German and mediaeval poetry.

The editor, Dr. Heinz Kindermann, of the most recent edition of *Von Deutscher Art und Kunst,* calls Goethe's essay a hymn to Gothic architecture; it is even more a hymn to Erwin Steinbach, one of the architects of Strassburg cathedral, and perhaps even more to the growing national pride. The title of the essay is *Von Deutsche Baukunst,* and two sentences are sufficient to show Goethe's nationalistic interest in mediaeval art. "Und nun soll ich nicht ergrimmen, heiliger Erwin, wenn der deutsche Kunstgelehrte auf Hörensagen neidischer Nachbarn seinen Vorzug verkennt, dein Werk mit unverstandnen Worte gotisch verkleinert. Da er Gott danken sollte, laut verkündigen zu können, das ist deutsche Baukunst, da der Italiener sich keiner eignen rühmen darf, viel weniger der Franzos." [2]

This work was carried on by many but particularly by Tieck and Wackenroder who together published in 1797 *Herzensergiessungen eines Kunstliebenden Klosterbruders* just before the latter's death. Tieck continued by publishing *Franz Sternbalds Wanderungen* and anthologies of mediaeval poetry and folksongs. He, in turn, was followed by the Brothers Grimm who collected fairy tales and folklore.

All the writings of the end of the century which admired or imitated the Middle Ages helped to an appreciation of Gothic architecture. But of all the group of the *ältere Romantiker,* the most influential in arousing an interest in mediaeval architecture was Friedrich Schlegel. He seems to have been the only one to take a definite interest in that

[2] *Von Deutscher Art und Kunst,* Deut. Litt. ed., p. 213.

art and to have made a special effort to study cathedrals while on his travels and to have emphasized the beauty of Gothic architecture in his writings. He even wrote a short book on Gothic architecture during his travels in 1804–5.

The title of his work was, *Principles of Gothic Architecture—notes of a Journey through the Netherlands, the Rhine Country, Switzerland and a part of France.* In it he writes, "I have a decided predilection for the Gothic style of architecture; and when I am so fortunate as to discover any monument, however ruined and defaced, I examine every portion of it with unwearied zeal and attention, for it appears to me that from a neglect of such study, the deep meaning and peculiar motive of Gothic architecture is seldom fully arrived at." [3]

In his last note on Gothic architecture, written after he returned to Paris, he writes, "On revisiting the Library, I found there, among many learned novelties and scientific treatises, one on Gothic architecture, by an Englishman. How strangely must the brains of some individuals be organized! This writer imagines himself to have made an entirely novel discovery, in tracing the foliated tree-like form of Gothic architecture, the lofty avenue-like aisles, leafy vaulting, and the universal similitude of every part to the vegetable productions of nature." [4] This quotation is worthy of note for it shows how closely the early ideas of Gothic were connected with the primeval forests and nature. The naturalism of Gothic was not superseded by the functionalism of Gothic until the middle of the century, but both interpretations are organic.

[3] *Schlegel's Aesthetic and Miscellaneous Works,* Bohm Lib. trans., p. 155.
[4] *Ibid.,* p. 193.

Schlegel in the concluding pages makes a few comments on the state of contemporary art. His attitude toward the reviving of the mediaeval styles is different from the contemporary feeling in England, and may explain why modern Gothic became popular in Germany so much later than in England. "How completely is this modern world shut out from all sense of the beautiful!" [5] ". . . no revival of art can take place until a grand improvement is seen in architectural designs . . ." "The romantic style of the middle ages may indeed be adopted in a few country houses as in England, where these miniature copies are seen in abundance; the materials exist, but the idea alone is wanting. We may yet erect churches in the glorious style of old Christian architecture, as rich in decoration and perhaps even more beautifully executed than those of other days; but the spirit of the times leads rather to the desecration and neglect of all the ancient houses of God than to incurring the expense and labor of building and endowing others." [6]

The person who did the most to divert the newly aroused enthusiasms of the Romantics toward Gothic architecture was Sulpiz Boisserée, who with his brother Melchior made careful drawings of the cathedral at Cologne. He also studied old manuscripts and drawings and so was able to make plans and studies of how the cathedral should be finished. Sulpiz was born in 1783. His parents died when he was ten. He lived with his grandmother in Cologne until 1800, when he went to Hamburg to study. During these early years he had played about the ruins of the cathedral and had grown very fond of it so that the drawings of the cathedral became the most important work of his life. In

[5] *Ibid.*, p. 198.   [6] *Ibid.*, p. 199.

1803 he went to Jena and later to Paris where he was with
the Schlegels and in the next year Friedrich Schlegel made
his trip in Belgium and Flanders in the company of Sulpiz
Boisserée, and it was from him that Schlegel derived his
interest in architecture. Sulpiz made most of the drawings
between 1807 and 1810 and then he travelled a great deal
to make people interested in the project of restoring and
completing the cathedral. In 1811 he was with Goethe in
Weimar. He saw the Crown Princes of Prussia and also of
Württemberg and in Berlin the architect Schinkel. By
1824 his great work was completed.[7] The German Academy
of Art recognized his work by making him a member, and
the University of Heidelberg gave him a Doctor of Philosophy in the class of architecture. King Frederick William
III sent him a gold snuff box. Through Boisserée's diligence and pertinacity many Germans were learning of
Gothic architecture.

However, the prevalent architectural style was classic,
and continued to be so until the 1840's. That great patron
of art, Ludwig of Bavaria, had classical buildings erected
in Munich with the exception of von Gartner's Italian Romanesque church. In Berlin most of the buildings were
classical also. The great Schinkel as early as 1819 made a
project for the cathedral in Berlin in a Gothic style, but it
was not accepted. In 1825, Schinkel made two designs for
the Werderkirche in Berlin and the Gothic plan was chosen
in preference to the classical. Most of Schinkel's buildings

[7] The diagrams and atlas of 18 plates were published at Stuttgart
in 1821. The text came out in 1823 at both Stuttgart and Paris under
the title, *Histoire et déscription de la cathédrale de Cologne, accompagnée de recherches sur l'architecture des anciennes cathédrales.*
The second, new revised and enlarged edition appeared in 1843 at
Munich.

were classical, but his paintings were romantic and he chose Gothic cathedrals and ruins for subject matter.

About 1812 there was a group of German painters who must be mentioned because they were a product of romanticism and to a great extent helped the cause of mediaeval art. They called themselves the Nazarenes or Christian painters and were greatly influenced by the Catholic revival which was part of the Romantic Movement. Most of them studied in Rome. They combined a classic style with Christian and romantic subjects. They often painted churches, cloisters and monks, as well as scenes from the Bible. Some of the best known of this group were Overbeck, Schadow, Veit and Schnorr. Their work helped to emphasize the religious aspects of art.

Another aspect of romanticism which aided the growing appreciation of mediaeval art was the patriotic nationalism which was becoming strong in the German States. The Napoleonic conquests set the scene for this patriotism. The speeches and writings of Fichte vocalized it. For several decades the sentiment had been growing stronger that the Germans had a glorious past. Baron Stein, who did so much to unite Germany against Napoleon, aided this sentiment by beginning the monumental compilation of old German documents, the *Monumenta Germaniae Historica,* to which work he devoted the last ten years of his life. Pertz continued the work and about it grew up a great school of German mediaeval historians.

In literature, the German school of romanticism was brilliant, prolific and shortlived. By 1833 when Heine wrote *Die Romantische Schule* in Paris, the movement was almost over. Friedrich Schlegel, Fichte, Novalis, Wackenroder, Arnim, Kleist, Hoffmann and Werner were all dead. Schleiermacher died during the following year. Which left only Tieck of the *ältere Romantiker* and Brentano and Uhland and Heine of the *jüngere Romantiker*. In this book Heine gives his definition of the Romantic School. "It was nothing else than the re-awakening of the poetry of the Middle Ages, in whatever manner it showed itself in lyrics, paintings and architecture, in Art and Life." [8] This shows quite clearly that one of the group at least recognized the importance of the Middle Ages as an inspiration of the romantic muse. It only seems strange that what had so clearly manifested itself in literature should have appeared so seldom in architecture.

Nine years after the publication of Heine's important book, in the autumn of 1842, the cornerstone of the new part of Cologne cathedral was laid. That dates the beginning of a widespread interest in Gothic architecture. The cornerstone was laid by the king Frederick William IV. It was a great affair and many dignitaries were present, and of course Sulpiz Boisserée whose drawings and zeal made the undertaking possible. The king greeted him with great enthusiasm and friendliness and said, "How many years have I known you? Twenty-nine years, since December 1813 in Frankfurt; yes, I now remember it very well, for three nights I could not sleep because of your drawings of the Cathedral." Alexander Humboldt reported that Metternich was quite disgusted by this display and remarked in French, "There is a mutual drunkenness there, which is perhaps more dangerous for the one who produces it than for the others." [9]

The restoration of the Cathedral which was begun in 1823 under Ahlert who died in 1833, continued under

[8] Heine, *Die Romantische Schule*, p. 2.
[9] Baur, *Geschichts- und Lebensbilder*, II: 352.

Zwirner until his death in 1861, and finally was finished under Voigtel in 1880, during which time many other architects worked there and so gained practical training in Gothic architecture. Most of these men are not very well known but they did original work in mediaeval styles. They are Statz, Schmidt, Schindz, Hofmann, Kuhn, Schneider and Marchang. Zwirner was the best known architect connected with the work and considered a great master of the Gothic style.

Another event which focussed the attention of German architects on the mediaeval styles of architecture was the open competition for the St. Nicholas church in Hamburg. In 1844 it was announced that the winning design was that of Gilbert Scott, the Englishman, who adapted the style of the late Romanesque, Rhenish churches. It was in the tradition of the national style, which is probably why Scott's plan was chosen, while that of the German, Semper, which was in the domed Byzantine style, received only second place. The result of this competition led to a greater appreciation of the national styles of mediaeval architecture and to an interest in the Gothic Revival in England. It also encouraged the use of modern Gothic throughout Germany and Austria.

The finest Gothic church of the nineteenth century built in a German-speaking country was the Votivkirche erected in Vienna between 1853 and 1879. It was designed by Heinrich von Ferstel and inspired by the thirteenth-century cathedrals. In Austria during the years 1850 and 1880 a number of churches were built in the Gothic style. In Hungary, the most notable example of nineteenth-century Gothic is the Parliament Building of Steindl in Budapest (1873–83).

During the second half of the nineteenth century buildings in a mediaeval style were erected in almost every part of Germany, save Baden which remained true to the classic tradition. Even Bavaria which had been the center of classicism under Ludwig I had a few notable examples of mediaevalizing. The first mediaeval style to be used there was the Italian Romanesque, but in the seventies von Riedel designed the National Museum in the English perpendicular style.

In Berlin the greatest number of modern Gothic buildings are to be found because it was a growing city which required new churches, and also was a wealthy center, as it became the capital of united Germany. We have already mentioned Schinkel's church designed in 1825. There was then an interval in which the classical styles flourished until 1844 when Friedrich August Stuler, who was the leading Berlin architect, designed the Jakobikirche. He designed many others in the Gothic styles in the next decade. Strack designed the Petrikirche in a fourteenth-century Gothic style in 1846. The great landmark was the Berlin Rathaus which was designed by Waesemann about 1860 in an Italian Romanesque manner. Several churches were designed by Adler in the 1860's in a Rhenish or Gothic style, but after 1865, in Berlin, the style degenerated into what is descriptively called the gingerbread Gothic, which was used particularly for villas.

Many other architects and many other buildings might be mentioned to show the extent of the interest in Gothic architecture in Germany. This interest had its greatest expression during the years from 1845 to 1870. Before the end of the century the new style of functionalism was started in Germany and Austria and comparatively few buildings in the mediaeval tradition were erected.

Modern Gothic was built extensively in Germany, but yet it had no revival comparable to that in England. One reason for that was that there was not such a strong religious revival to stimulate church building. Another was that there were not so many towns which grew so tremendously in population as there were in England. Nevertheless, the mediaeval styles came into vogue and stemmed the current of classicism which had been prevalent at the beginning of the century; and today in Germany there are many Gothic buildings which date from the nineteenth century.

In trying to sum up the spread of modern Gothic in Germany, it is perhaps interesting to quote the words of a French architect, Félix Narjoux, who travelled in north Germany in 1874, and who made a special study of the new Gothic buildings in Hanover and Hamburg.

Narjoux was an architect of standing in the Second Empire and Third Republic in France. Gothic architecture was one of his specialties and he did reconstructions, as well as original work. He was a pupil of Viollet-le-Duc, and later collaborated with him in writing *Habitations modernes en Europe*. His remarks on modern German Gothic should be authoritative.

"The Germans, as we have already said, have never had any architecture peculiar to themselves; they take their ideas from the buildings of foreign countries, and copy those of past ages. The types of Gothic architecture which they possess are far inferior to the magnificent examples of the Middle Ages to be found in France; and they did not dream of reviving this style in Germany till after the appearance of those buildings which were the results of our first archaeological studies, which, twenty-five years ago, led us to regard with honor edifices till then considered rude and barbarous. They followed in our steps, profiting by our attempts, our studies, and our faults; translating into their language, without compunction, extracts from our works, in order to apply the results of our researches. And in the same manner as the Germans who built the cathedral at Cologne knew and imitated those of Amiens, Beauvais and Troyes, so modern Germans, finding in a neighboring country information, hints, and formulae ready to their hand, have, with great skill and much success, appropriated to themselves all that could be useful and profitable. But while, amongst ourselves, the architects of the Gothic school limited their works to the restoration of ancient buildings and to the construction of churches, the Germans, on the contrary, went farther, and following out the ideas which they had received, erected ecclesiastical and civil structures, both public and private, said to be Gothic, in which, while they respected the fundamental principles of the logical reasoning which had served as a basis and starting-point, they varied the forms and multiplied their combinations, so as to obtain different results, and to carry out varied plans suited to all the requirements of public and private life. Their want of imagination in works of art was of service instead of hindrance to them in the laborious task from which they derived such excellent results. . . . As to our influence in the country, it is latent, but incontestable; facts prove it, though not a single German has had the good taste to allow or own it." [10]

M. Narjoux has endeavored to be impartial. He has praise for the modern Gothic in Germany, and repeats that nothing comparable had been built in France. But the na-

[10] Narjoux, *A Journey of an Architect,* pp. 250-2.

tionalistic spirit of the time makes him consider France the inspiration of the new style. It is true that the Germans did make use of the architectural studies of the French mediaeval archaeologists. But as we survey the scene sixty years later, it is apparent that the French played a minor role in forming modern Gothic in Germany.

The first appreciation of *die deutsche Baukunst* was as early as the 1770's in the works of Herder and Goethe. It was one of the manifestations of the Romantic School in Germany and was inextricably connected with the growth of national pride and patriotic sentiments, which was another dominating feature of German romanticism. It is true that very few Gothic buildings were erected during the Romantic period. That is not surprising, for it takes about a generation for new ideas to filter through society and to become acceptable to the conservatives. Even by 1833, the ideas of the romantic writers made themselves manifest in the Frankfort uprising. Since this attempt was unsuccessful and the rights of the estates in Germany were further curtailed by the resolutions of Teplitz and Vienna, the ideal of national unity and independence was driven underground, but it did not die out, but only grew stronger and more widespread, so that in 1848, there were uprisings all over Germany which resulted in the revised Constitution of 1849.

As the nationalistic feeling grew in the German states, so spread the vogue for modern Gothic, and the style was most extensively used in the period of national development, from 1848 to 1871. To the historian, the Gothic Revival in Germany is of particular interest, for it so closely parallels the growth of nationalism.

CHAPTER VI

THE GOTHIC REVIVAL IN THE UNITED STATES

ARCHITECTURE in colonial America followed closely the styles of Europe. Not yet is there a distinctive American style, although there are certain types of buildings in America which are not to be found in Europe such as the skyscrapers and the frame summer cottages, but they are designed to meet social needs and have no original architectural style as yet. Architecture in colonial America was not uniform but exhibited the national differences of the settlers. In the southwest and along the Pacific coast, the Spaniards built in styles analogous to the contemporary ones in Spain from the sixteenth century on. In the Thirteen Colonies which were settled by the English, the architectural styles employed were similar to those in England. In the church of St. Luke's in Smithfield, Virginia, the general design with the square tower and pointed windows is Gothic because at that time, about 1632, Gothic was still used for parish churches in England. Some of the frame buildings in New England, like the Whipple House in Salem, have projecting upper storeys like the mediaeval houses in Europe. Classic details which had been introduced into England by Inigo Jones were also introduced into the colonial buildings. The later edifices were still similar to the English styles of Queen Anne and the Georges. The ornament of colonial houses was Palladian

130

because that was the approved style in England before 1776.

There was a fad for Gothic ornament in England about 1750 which culminated in the Gothicizing of Strawberry Hill by Sir Horace Walpole. That vogue had few repercussions in the Colonies. Nevertheless Thomas Jefferson, that well-read, well-travelled, Virginian aristocrat, seems to have been one of the few colonials to have turned his versatile attention to the Gothicizing fashion and toyed with the idea of a Gothic temple for his garden. As early as 1771, among his notes for a "Burying Place" at Monticello, is the sentence: "In the center of it erect a small Gothic temple of antique appearance." [1] In a memo for the gardens in 1804 he again mentions a Gothic Temple,[2] and in 1807 he even made a small sketch of a ground plan with the following memo, "A gothic temple or rather portico . . . resembling that in Meinhert, p. 137." [3] Bricks were ordered for this gothicism on December 15, 1807.[4] These were but whims and fancies, for his true love was the Maison Carrée at Nimes. Jefferson was always much interested in architecture. He owned a fair sized architectural library and made architectural designs, the best known of which are those for Monticello, the capitol of Virginia at Richmond, and the buildings for the University of Virginia. He favored the use of classical styles, especially Roman, since Rome had been a republic, as the most fitting for the United States and most in harmony with the ideals of the new country.

[1] Randall, *Life of Jefferson*, I:60.
[2] *Thomas Jefferson, Architect*, MS reproduced in facsimile No. 161.
[3] *Ibid.*, No. 165.
[4] Kimball, essay in *Thomas Jefferson, Architect*, p. 169.

It was not until the early Republic that any buildings
were designed or erected in the Gothic manner. The first
architect to use the style was Benjamin Henry Latrobe who
had studied in England and Germany and is best known for
his classical work. He was primarily an architect of the
Greek Revival and his best work was the Second United
States Bank in Philadelphia in which he adopted the octa-
style Doric form of the Parthenon itself.[5] Twenty years
earlier, however, in 1799 he designed the Gothic mansion
of Sedgeley outside Philadelphia.[6] In 1805 he submitted
two designs for the Catholic Cathedral in Baltimore. One
was Gothic, but the other, the classical design, was accepted. About the same time, 1807, the French architect,
Godefroy, who worked with Latrobe, designed the chapel
of Saint Mary's Seminary in Baltimore, which has a Gothic
façade.

The Greek Revival had more immediate success than the
Gothic Revival, but after 1820 various churches were built
of wood, with Gothic details. This frame construction with
mediaeval ornament generally goes by the name of Car-
penters' Gothic. For more than twenty years churches
were built in this manner. A good example of the early
thirties is the frame First Parish Church, north of Harvard
Square in Cambridge, Massachusetts. Dwelling houses
were also designed in this manner and there are still a few
of these wooden houses with gables and pinnacles to be
seen in New England.

One of the first American architects to work almost ex-

[5] Latrobe began the plans and buildings in 1819. He died the
following year and his pupil William Strickland carried on the work
which was completed in 1824.

[6] T. Westcott, *Historic Mansions and Buildings of Philadelphia*,
p. 449 ff.

clusively in the Gothic manner was Alexander Jackson
Davis who lived from 1803 to 1882. He was an excellent
draughtsman, but had no formal architectural training. He
designed several churches, but most of his work was collegiate and domestic. One of the first houses which he designed was Glenn Ellen, just outside Baltimore, for the Gil-
mor family. It was begun in 1832 and was supposed to be a
copy of Sir Walter Scott's Abbotsford. It is now deserted
and ruined. Another house which Davis designed quite
early in his career and which is still inhabited and in good
repair is the Rotch House in New Bedford which was begun
in 1836.

Davis's first civic building of note was the New York
University building which was erected on Washington
Square between 1833–36. It had a very pleasing façade
with a crenelated skyline, towers and turrets, and a large
Gothic window over the main entrance. It was probably
the first civic building in the Gothic manner to be erected
in New York. One of the most ambitious buildings which
he designed in New York was the House of Mansions at
41st and Fifth Avenue. He also made designs for Michigan
University and the Virginia Military Institute.

His most effective buildings were country mansions.
Washington Irving, who was one of the few American writers of the Romantic School, encouraged the fashion which
made Gothic villas so popular, by converting his house,
"Sunnyside," into a picturesque Tudor villa. While Davis
did not work on Irving's house, he did design many in the
neighborhood. By the end of the thirties many wealthy
New Yorkers wished to have a country house not too far
away from the city. A good number of them chose the
banks of the Hudson about Tarrytown which Irving was

making so popular by his writings. The style usually chosen for these houses was Gothic.

One reason that the country houses of the forties and fifties were usually mediaeval in decoration was the popularity of a book written by Andrew Downing in 1841. Like so many books of the period the title is long enough to be a short résumé. It runs as follows: *A Treatise on the Theory and Practice of Landscape Gardening, Adapted to North America; with a View to the Improvement of Country Residences. Comprising Historical Notices and General Principles of the Art, Directions for Laying Out Grounds and Arranging Plantations, the Description and Cultivation of Hardy Trees, Decorative Accompaniments to the House and Grounds, the Formation of Pieces of Artificial Water, Flower Gardens, etc., with Remarks on Rural Architecture.* From this encyclopedic volume, the wealthy merchants learned the value of the picturesque and the charm of Gothic villas. The illustrations were by Davis, and as the work was much read, it is not surprising that Davis received many commissions to design Hudson River Gothic.

One of the first of these houses which Davis designed was the Paulding House at Irvington-on-Hudson. The first plans were made in 1838. Philip Hone, a fashionable gentleman who kept a good diary, saw it in July, 1841 and commented on it. "In the course of our drive we went to see Mr. William Paulding's magnificent house, yet unfinished, on the Bank below Tarrytown. It is an immense edifice of white or gray marble, resembling a baronial castle, or rather a Gothic monastery, with towers, turrets, and trellises; minarets, mosaics, and mouseholes: archways, armories, and airholes; peaked windows and pinnacled roofs, and many other fantastics too tedious to enumerate, the whole constituting an edifice of gigantic size, with no room in it; great cost and little comfort, which if I mistake not, will one of these days be designated as 'Paulding's Folly.' " [7]

The vogue for the Gothic which permeated the United States in the forties was similar to that which had flourished in England about 1820 and in France about 1830. It was not restricted to one part of the country or to one architect; nor did it manifest itself only in architecture, but also in furniture and interior decoration. Chairs and tables similar to those which Pugin designed for Windsor in 1827 were made in Boston and New York. The American designers got most of their ideas from the English books of plates such as Pugin's, Britton's and Ackerman's *Repository*. This Gothic vogue was directly imported from England as the classical had been during the colonial period. Lamps and desk sets of Brummagem Gothic were imported as well as Gothic wallpapers. The architects used the English books of designs as well as the cabinet makers. Robinson's *Rural Architecture* was the source of inspiration for many of the Gothic houses in the United States.

About 1840, also, the principles of the English Gothic Revival influenced church architecture in America. Those tenets were archaeological correctness, sound construction and liturgical fitness. The first churches built according to these principles were in New York. The earliest was Trinity Church, designed by Richard Upjohn and built between 1839–46. It meticulously followed English models and in turn became a model for innumerable churches in the United States. Upjohn designed many other churches and founded an American architectural family which is noted for its ecclesiastical building.

[7] Philip Hone, *Diary*, II:550.

The other New York church which early expressed the Gothic Revival principles was Grace Church, built between 1843–46, and designed by James Renwick, who was another noted church architect of the middle of the century. His most famous building is St. Patrick's Cathedral in New York, 1850–79. In this he did not follow English Gothic, but even as the contemporary English Revivalists were doing, he sought his inspiration in French cathedrals.

The classic tradition remained much stronger in civic building. Of all the state capitols which were built before the Civil War the only one which was in the Gothic tradition was that of Louisiana at Baton Rouge designed by Dakin. In Washington the classic tradition continued until the building of the Smithsonian Institute which was built in the fifties in a style which was evidently derived from the Romanesque.[8] One reason for the choice of this unusual style was the personal taste of Robert Dale Owen who was the chairman of the Building Committee. He admired the mediaeval styles and felt that they could be adapted to current needs. He wrote a book explaining his point of view. It was published in 1849 and was widely read and had a definite influence on civic building in the third quarter of the century. It was entitled, *Hints on Public Architecture, Containing, among Other Illustrations, Views and Plans of the Smithsonian Institution; together with an Appendix Relative to Building Materials.* In this he advocated the mediaeval styles on all grounds, including that of economy. He seems to have been read with attention, for a number of town halls, court houses, libraries and police courts were built in the mediaeval manner.

The sixties in America did not witness much building

[8] Designed by James Renwick.

because of the Civil War and the depressed economic condition which followed it. The writings of John Ruskin had been read in the United States before the war but they did not bear fruit until after it. Then his moral aesthetics became more popular, and the use of the Italian mediaeval styles. Buildings were erected according to his principles, which were typical specimens of Victorian Gothic and were no more pleasing than the contemporary buildings in England. Red brick was the material most often used. One of the most noted buildings of this period is Memorial Hall at Harvard University, designed by Wade and built between 1870–77. Another which was admired in its day was the Philadelphia Academy of Fine Arts, erected in 1876.

The Centennial Exposition held in Philadelphia in 1876 had a stimulating effect on building. The general effect, however, was only toward a greater eclecticism. Two main currents became discernible. One was led by Richard Hunt who was one of the first American architects to have a Beaux Arts training. That School was always conservative and at that time was favoring French Renaissance styles, which Hunt introduced with great success into the United States.

The other tendency was the Romanesque Revival of which H. H. Richardson was the leader and main exponent. His most noted work was Trinity Church in Boston, which was begun in 1872. All the buildings which he designed, penitentiaries, libraries or churches, were in this style. He was much admired and is still considered one of the foremost American architects. His last building was the Allegheny Court House in Pittsburgh, which was begun in 1884 and was also in the French Romanesque style. He died at the age of forty-eight in 1886, and had but few followers to carry on the style.

Another stepping stone in American architectural history was the Columbian Exposition in Chicago in 1893. The original designs by Root were in the Richardson tradition of the Romanesque Revival. Root died suddenly before they were completed and the new group of men, of which Burnham, Atkinson and Sullivan were the most prominent, were partisans of the classic tradition or of the new principles of functionalism which were coming into vogue with the new building materials of steel and concrete.

Nevertheless, the Gothic did not die out in the United States. It had been used almost exclusively in ecclesiastical architecture since the forties, and its use was continued. The continuation of the Gothic tradition until the present day in America is due in large measure to the work of two men. One was Henry Adams who wrote *Mont St. Michel and Chartres.*[9] That book, although it has not been available in a cheap edition until 1936, has been greatly influential in making Americans appreciate and love French Gothic. It started a cult for the French mediaeval architecture similar to that started by Ruskin for the Italian. The other man is Ralph Adams Cram.

Mr. Cram has been most influential in keeping alive an appreciation of Gothic architecture, both by his writings and his buildings. His first church which was designed with Goodhue was the All Saints Chapel in Ashmont, Massachusetts, which was begun in 1892. At that time the vogue for the Romanesque was dying out and there was a strong reaction against Victorian Gothic. The plan of this church

[9] Privately printed, 1905.

was simple, based on that of an English parish church with large pointed windows filled with modified perpendicular tracery. It was built of local stone which had a yellowish orange hue. The exterior was strong and imposing with a low square tower. Innumerable suburban churches have been built in the same manner, for it was much admired.

The next important work which Cram and Goodhue undertook were the new buildings of the Military Academy at West Point. They won the competition in which seven firms had been invited to compete. The other firms were working in the classical and Renaissance styles which had become popular about 1900. Some of the old buildings [10] at West Point had been in the Gothic manner and a certain conservative group were in favor of continuing the tradition. Cram felt that Gothic was appropriate to the picturesque scenery of the Hudson, just as the builders of the Gothic mansions had felt sixty years earlier. The plans were made in 1903 and show the characteristics which are typical of Cram's work. He read Viollet-le-Duc with attention on the structural principles of Gothic, but he did not try to be archaeological in his designs. He had a native ability to design in mass and little interest in decorative detail, which makes his work so different from that of the early Gothic Revivalists who were primarily interested in detail and ornament. The buildings at West Point are massive

[10] The first buildings at West Point, built between 1820–30, were classic. About 1850 the Gothic style was used for the Central Barracks, Library, etc. About 1898, McKim, Mead and White designed McCullum Hall and the adjoining buildings in a classic style. The success of the plans and buildings of Cram, Goodhue & Ferguson in the late Gothic style have fixed that as the traditional style in West Point. Therefore, the five new buildings which are being designed by Paul Cret, at present, are to be in the Gothic tradition. (Information given by M. Paul Cret.)

and simple and give an impression of strength owing to the rough dressing of the large blocks of stone. The facings of the windows and doors are simple.

The buildings at West Point are but one example of the twentieth century vogue for "college Gothic," which may be considered to have started with the designs of Henry Ives Cobb for the University of Chicago about 1891. Soon after Cope and Stewardson designed the dormitories at the University of Pennsylvania and Bryn Mawr, and Day and Klauder the dormitories at Princeton. James Gamble Rogers, who designed Harkness at Yale, is another architect who has furthered academic Gothic. Other examples of which are to be found at Princeton in the Chapel and the Graduate College, which were designed by Cram; and in the later buildings at Bryn Mawr for which Cram was consultant architect. For about a century, mediaeval styles have been favored for academic buildings. The English tradition of mediaeval styles at Oxford and Cambridge are probably in large measure responsible for this. We have already noted the Gothic building of New York University designed by Davis in 1833. Intermediate examples are the buildings (College Hall, Logan Hall and the Hospital) designed by Richards about 1870 for the University of Pennsylvania in Philadelphia. The mediaeval tradition for colleges continues into the present, but the style has changed to be adaptable to the steel and concrete.fireproof construction. The exterior is generally faced with pink brick and the facings of white limestone. The general impression is Tudor while the details are thirteenth or fourteenth century in inspiration. A recent example of this style is the Science Building at Wellesley College, Wellesley, Massachusetts, which was built between 1934–36.

Cram has designed a number of churches. One of his greatest designs is that for the Cathedral of St. John the Divine in New York, accepted in 1927. The cathedral is still under construction. Another of his churches is the Swedenborgian Cathedral Church at Bryn Athyn, Pennsylvania. In it, he has been influenced by French mediaeval architecture. The cloisters and the separate bell-tower are Romanesque; the choir is early Gothic and the nave is later. Many churches in France exhibit the same mixture of styles because they were built during centuries. This was a definite attempt to reproduce the Middle Ages in America, and they even tried to gather a group of skilled masons and stone carvers who would make their own designs for corbels, capitals and voussoirs. Since it was almost impossible to get men who could design as well as carve, the work has gone very slowly.

The Episcopal Cathedral in Washington is another example of a great Gothic building in America which is trying to reproduce the feeling and enthusiasms of the Middle Ages. The work there is going slowly, also, and there is meticulous attention to detail. A mediaeval art which has been greatly stimulated by these new cathedral buildings is that of stained glass. John La Farge (1835–1910) was the forerunner of this American school of stained glass. He was a great admirer of mediaeval glass but most of his designs do not show this influence. He experimented in glass making and invented the opalescent glass which had a great vogue in the last quarter of the nineteenth century. The twentieth-century glass designers tried even more faithfully to reproduce the color and the technique of twelfth-century windows, especially those of Chartres. One of the best known studios at present is that of Nicolas d'Ascenzo in Philadelphia, but there are many others which are continuing the mediaeval tradition.

More buildings in the Gothic manner have been built in the United States than in any other country in the nineteenth and twentieth centuries, which of course is only natural since it was a newly settled country which required new buildings. Gothic was first used most extensively in domestic architecture, and then became the accepted style for academic buildings and churches. There have been comparatively few industrial or business buildings in the mediaeval styles. Gothic details have been added to skyscrapers. The most notable example of the adaptation of the Gothic to an office building was one of the first skyscrapers in New York. It is the Woolworth Building which was designed by Cass Gilbert and built between 1911–13. The elevation is that of a Gothic cathedral with a tower 779 feet high. The vertical effect is emphasized by the arrangement of windows in vertical bands which give it surprising lightness and carry out the general appearance of a Gothic cathedral.

Since America was not settled until the Middle Ages were well over, it may seem strange that there has been so much building in the Gothic manner. It shows conclusively how the artistic development of America has been closely affiliated with that of Europe and particularly that of England and France. At the present time the Gothic tradition is strongest in the country where there was no mediaeval Gothic architecture.

It is for that reason that the Swedenborgian Cathedral at Bryn Athyn has been chosen for the frontispiece. It is the fullest and most successful expression of the Gothic Revival. It unites the aims and aspirations of Pugin, the

Ecclesiologists, Ruskin, Scott, Viollet-le-Duc and Zwirner, all that is best of the nineteenth-century Revivalists. Nothing shows better how we have progressed in love and knowledge of the Middle Ages. This can best be expressed by Cram's own words. "I seemed to see here a chance to put into practice some of my theories of a Mediaeval guild system, and the idea was cordially received. What I tried to do was to make all the workmen of every sort joint partners with the architects in producing a building that should be wholly personal in its structural qualities and its craftsmanship, and also to establish, all around the projected cathedral, workshops and studios for the production of sculpture and stone-carving, cabinetwork and joinery, metalwork and stained glass . . . the result is not only unique but one of the most picturesque and romantic architectural compositions in the country. It is a sort of epitome of English church-building from the earliest Norman to the latest Perpendicular; learned, scholarly, poetic; a real masterpiece of reminiscent yet creative art." [11]

[11] Cram, *My Life in Architecture*, pp. 248–50.

Chapter VII

ROMANTICISM AND THE GOTHIC REVIVAL

IF THERE had been no Romantic Movement, there would have been no Gothic Revival. If the classic spirit, which is content with gradual and continuous growth, had continued throughout the eighteenth century, the architectural style of the nineteenth century would have been modified Renaissance. But as romanticism, with its spirit of discontent and love of change, disrupted the natural evolution of history and architectural styles, the nineteenth century resulted in a period of eclecticism. The two most important styles of the Romantic period were connected with the two dominating ideals of the nineteenth century, democracy and nationalism. The Greek Revival was the expression of the former, and the Gothic Revival of the latter. And even as democratic idealism was in large measure superseded by imperialistic nationalism, so the Greek Revival was followed by the Gothic Revival.

The whole history of the Gothic Revival in England from the time of Batty Langley until the present is closely connected with the history of romanticism. No architectural style has been less associated with aesthetics and abstract principles of art. That would require more objectivity than is compatible with the romantic spirit.

In the eighteenth century the artistic interest in the Gothic was confined to decoration. At that time it was almost wholly divorced from Christianity. It was used for

144

garden architecture and for dwellings. What could be more romantic than a sham ruin when romantic was defined as fantastic and fictitious?

Nothing is more displeasing to a classicist than a ruin, for he enjoys the completed whole. On the other hand, nothing is more pleasing to the romantic temperament, which likes the unfinished, the incomplete, for then there is always the possibility of change. The following quotations well express the romantic attitude. The first was written by Shenstone in the middle of the eighteenth century, and the second by A. J. Downing in the middle of the nineteenth.

"Ruinated structures appear to derive their power of pleasing from the irregularity of surface which is variety; and the latitude they afford the imagination to conceive an enlargement of their dimensions, or to recollect any events, or circumstances appertaining to their pristine grandeur and solemnity." [1]

"It is but a mile from Newport to Carisbrook Castle, one of the most interesting old Ruins in England. It crowns a fine hill, and from the top of its ruined towers, you look over a lovely landscape of hill and vale, picturesque villages, and green meadows. The castle, itself, with its fortifications, covers perhaps half a dozen acres, and is just in that state of ruin and decay, best calculated to excite the imagination, and send one upon a voyage into dreamland." [2]

The eighteenth century was looking for something different rather than something new. It was not so interested in creation, as in adaptation. Therefore any artistic style which had been used before or elsewhere was pleasing. It

---

[1] Shenstone, *Essays on Men and Manners*, p. 67.
[2] Downing, *Rural Essays*, p. 525.

was a century of talent rather than of genius; an age of refinement rather than of innovation. The Adam brothers
refined Roman art and Batty Langley attempted to refine
the Gothic. There was some scholarship, but more dilet-
tantism. Eighteenth-century Gothic reflects all these characteristics.

A stanza from the *Lay of the Last Minstrel* by Sir Walter Scott sums up the purely romantic approach to the
appreciation of a mediaeval building. The subjective, emotional reaction is of paramount importance, therefore,—

> "If thou would'st view fair Melrose aright,
> Go visit it by the pale moonlight;
> For the gay beams of lightsome day
> Gild, but to flout, the ruins gray." [3]

About 1820 the attitude toward the Gothic changed. The
architects, at least, instead of looking at the old buildings
sentimentally began studying them carefully. The archaeological approach followed the emotional; instead of hiding
the outlines of a Gothic building in trees and shrubs, they
began drawing them mathematically to scale. The sentimental attitude has not completely died out even today and
it continued throughout the last century. A. W. Pugin gives
a good description of the tourist of about 1835. ". . . the
third class are persons who go to see the church. They are
tourists; They go to see everything that is to be seen; therefore they see the church,—*id est,* they walk round, read the
epitaphs, think it very pretty, very romantic, very old, suppose that it was built in superstitious times, pace the length
of the nave, write their names on a pillar, and whisk out, as
they have a great deal more to see and very little time." [4]

[3] Scott, *Lay of the Last Minstrel,* Canto II, st. 1.
[4] Pugin, *Contrasts,* p. 36.

Nevertheless, the archaeological and scientific interest in Gothic was beginning among a small group as early as 1820. The elder Pugin was drawing Gothic details to a mathematical scale. At the same time Rickman was trying to give a stylistic label to each phase of mediaeval building. The purely emotional appreciation of the Gothic was being replaced by a more minute and painstaking study of the architectural remains of the Middle Ages.

About a decade later in England there was a wave of religious feeling which manifested itself in various ways. Perhaps most important were the Tractarians at Oxford and the Ecclesiologists at Cambridge. Both felt that the only way to improve divine worship was to improve church planning, and that by making churches conform to the liturgy and rubrics, the services would naturally improve. The only known type of architecture which conformed to the old usage was the Gothic. Hence they advocated the revival of Gothic for religious reasons, and in the '40's a moral consideration was added to the appreciation of the Gothic.

It may seem strange that the Romanticists were content with the Gothic instead of creating a new style. But the eighteenth century did not want anything completely original, merely adaptations of many different styles. Chambers built a Chinese pagoda with gilt dragons in Kew Gardens. It was as much admired and marvelled at as Walpole's Gothic Strawberry Hill or the classical façades and interiors of the Adams.

> "Variety's the very spice of life
> That gives it all its flavour." [5]

Those lines from *The Task* by Cowper, published in 1785,

[5] Cowper, *The Task*, Bk. 2, l. 606.

might well be the motto of the second half of the eighteenth century.

By the early nineteenth century and the beginning of the Romantic Movement, the Gothic had come to symbolize certain of the aims and aspirations of the period. No new art could have been more symbolic, more expressive of the nineteenth-century manifestation of the romantic spirit. Gothic was non-classical, closely connected with Christianity, with national history. It appeared to be fantastic, imaginative, irrational and emotional. They saw in it the reproduction in stone of the primeval forests. Almost every aspect of their new attitude toward art and life they saw in Gothic architecture. Therefore, naturally, the architects did not attempt to create a new style when an old one would most perfectly fit the taste of their clients. The Middle Ages as seen through romantic spectacles seemed very good to most people and they were content to have a Gothical house to live in, and later in the century, people felt morally better to worship in an Early Decorated church. No other architectural style would have suited the mediaevalists, so there had to be a Gothic Revival. An etching by Pugin well sums up one attitude of the period: one Gothic cathedral is worth more than ten Renaissance buildings: "They were weighed in the balance and found wanting."

In England the Gothic Revival was not dependent on the literature of the Romantic Movement to any great extent, for none of the greatest of the School, except Walter Scott, were interested in the Middle Ages. The reason for that was that Shakespeare and early ballads were no novelty to the English as they were to the Germans and French. In England, there had been no far-reaching classicism to stamp out the late mediaeval literature. Even in the

Augustan Age Spenser was read and admired. Therefore the English Romantics, in their quest for change, could not turn to the authors whose work was always read. Instead, Wordsworth received mystic inspiration from Nature, Shelley and Keats from antique Greece, and Byron from the Orient. In England, there were two phases of the Gothic Revival: the secular revival of the eighteenth century which was more closely connected with the literature of the period; and the ecclesiastical revival of the nineteenth century which was connected with the reform of the Anglican church.

In France the literature of the Romantic Movement was more important in forming an interest in Gothic architecture, especially Chateaubriand's *Le Génie,* and Hugo's *Notre Dame.* But the classic tradition was so strong in France that they could not accept modern Gothic as a usable style, but contented themselves by restoring the mediaeval monuments, by archaeology and history.

In Germany, the spirit of the literature of the Romantic Movement and that which animated the building of modern Gothic, seem to be most closely connected, for both express the coming nationalism.

The Gothic Revival in the United States is an importation from England. At first it seems most incongruous, for it has not even the excuse of being a reminder of former national greatness. On reflection, both the Gothic Revival and the eclecticism of American architecture are seen to be true expressions of American history. The Colonies became a nation in the Romantic period, and romantic ideas were in large measure responsible for the formation of American ideals. The keynote of American civilization was given in the often quoted words of Thomas Jefferson in the

Declaration of Independence. "We hold these truths to be self-evident that all men are created equal; that they are endowed by their Creator with certain inalienable rights, that among these are life, liberty and pursuit of happiness." That sentence might be called the epitome of romantic political thought, and it has molded the attitude of the citizens of the United States to the present day, and most especially that of the immigrants. It is by recognition of the fundamental romanticism of the United States that the present inconsistencies in its civilization become understandable. Love of change might better be the motto of the United States than *e pluribus unum.* So if this romantic attitude be accepted, it is not surprising that the romantic style of the Gothic Revival flourishes in the United States.

The most reiterated criticism of Gothic Revival architecture runs as follows: Architecture must conform to the spirit of the time in which it is built. It must conform to the main characteristics of the age in material, construction and design. The nineteenth century was an age of mechanical inventions, of the growth of democratic theory in government, of trade and industry, of materialism and agnosticism. It was as completely different from the Middle Ages as was possible in government, social conditions and religious feeling. Therefore every building of the Gothic Revival was false to the spirit of the age, and in consequence cannot be considered as good architecture. This criticism has grown out of a one-sided interpretation of the nineteenth century. It ignores the importance of the Romantic Movement.

As early as 1870 when Eastlake was writing his *History of the Gothic Revival,* people were beginning to feel that it was incongruous to erect buildings in a Gothic style in the nineteenth century. Eastlake, himself, writes, "At first it may seem strange that a style of design which is intimately associated with the romance of the world's history should now-a-days find favour in a country distinguished above all others for the plain business-like tenour of its daily life." [6] And at heart, although he was a Gothic Revivalist, he did find it strange.

But thirty years earlier, when Pugin was writing his *Apology for the Revival of Christian Architecture in England*, the Gothic Revival was at its strongest and no such doubt of its fitness had entered his mind. He wrote as follows: "It will not be difficult to show that the wants and purposes of Civil Buildings now are almost identical with those of our English forefathers. In the first place, climate, which necessarily regulates the pitch of roofs, light, warmth, and internal arrangement, remains of course precisely the same as formerly. Secondly, we are governed by nearly the same laws and the same system of political economy. The Sovereign, with the officers of state connected with the crown,—the Houses of Peers and Commons,— the judges of the various courts of law, and form of trial,— the titles and rank of the nobility,—the tenures by which their lands are held, and the privileges they enjoy,—the corporate bodies and civic functionaries,—are all essentially the same as in former days. There is no country in Europe which has preserved so much of her ancient system as England." [7]

These two quotations shows the difference in attitude toward the Gothic Revival even during the nineteenth century. So long as the spirit of the Romantic Movement was prevalent, the Gothic Revival expressed the spirit of

[6] Eastlake, *op. cit.*, p. 2.   [7] A. W. Pugin, *Apology,* p. 37.

romanticism. But later, when that spirit was almost crushed out by Victorian materialism, the Gothic Revival was no longer a vital style and it did seem strange that England should be dotted with modern Gothic buildings.

But whether current taste says that the Gothic Revival is good or bad, it is at least one of the most lasting and tangible legacies of the Romantic Movement, and shows that the nineteenth century was not completely engrossed by Progress, Industry, Science and the Future, but, also, looked backward to discover the Middle Ages.

GLOSSARY OF TERMS
Used to Describe Post-Renaissance Gothic

ENGLAND

Batty-Langley manner, 1745–55
Thomas Gray uses this term in a letter dated August 13, 1754.

Chippendale Gothic, c. 1750
Used exclusively for furniture.

Strawberry Hill Gothick, 1755–1765
Sometimes used to describe all eighteenth-century English Gothic. Richard Bentley was the best designer in this style.

Gothicizing Style, 1750–1800
The fashion of adding Gothic decoration to Georgian buildings.

Castellated Gothic, 1800–1830
Domestic architecture modelled on mediaeval castles. Wyatt and his nephew Wyatville were foremost architects of this style.

Cardboard Gothic, 1810–1830
Term applied to Commissioners' Churches in the Gothic style.

Brummagem Gothic, 1820–1840
A. W. Pugin, "True Principles," p. 22. Gothic decoration and household ornaments made with moulds, either of cast iron or plaster. Mostly manufactured in Birmingham, hence the name.

Gothic Revival
  a. General usage: to describe all artistic work inspired by the art of the Middle Ages since the Renaissance. Usually refers to England, but has been applied to all countries.
  b. Specific usage: Church architecture in England from 1820–1870 built according to the principles of (1) archaeological correctness of style, (2) logical, organic construction, (3) liturgical fitness and propriety, with chancel and choir screen. Best examples date about 1850 and are the works of A. W. Pugin, G. G. Scott and J. L. Pearson.

Streaky-bacon Style, 1860–1880
Buildings of varied colored brick inspired by Venetian Gothic and Italian Romanesque and the writings of John Ruskin.

153

Victorian Gothic, 1851–1900

An eclectic style based on all periods of mediaeval architecture of all countries. A mixture of pure Gothic Revival and Ruskinism. Used mostly in urban building, both civic and domestic. The building materials generally employed were: varied colored brick, particularly a deep crimson which becomes purplish in a smoky city, and orangish red terracotta. An ornate style with floriated detail and irregular skyline.

Original Gothic, 1890 to date

Based on the principles of mediaeval construction to be found in Viollet-le-Duc's *Dictionary*. Theoretically but not archaeologically true to mediaeval Gothic. The results are generally reminiscent of thirteenth-century French cathedrals. Liverpool Cathedral is the most noted example.

UNITED STATES

Carpenters' Gothic, 1820–1840

Term given to all early nineteenth-century frame buildings with Gothic ornament.

Hudson River Gothic, 1840–1860

Country mansions and suburban villas based on English models of the castellated or picturesque styles.

Ruskin Gothic, 1870–1890

Buildings based on English models which in turn had been inspired by mediaeval Italian architecture.

Romanesque Revival, 1872–1893

Work done by H. H. Richardson or his followers.

Gingerbread Gothic, 1880–1900

Private dwellings with very ornate exteriors covered with pinnacles, cupolas and dormers, and elaborately decorated with cast iron filigree.

Collegiate Gothic or College Gothic, 1900 to date

Two main styles. One based on English Perpendicular and built of large roughly dressed stones: example, Chapel, Princeton. The other based on English Tudor and built with steel construction and brick facing: example, Bennett Hall, University of Pennsylvania.

Modern Gothic, 1892 to date

Term applied to ecclesiastical building which follows the spirit but not the letter of the mediaeval Gothic. The most noted architect of this style is Ralph Adams Cram.

IN ALL COUNTRIES

Romanticism

Recent writers of architectural history in all countries recognize the modern buildings in mediaeval styles. The term generally given to this architecture is Romanticism because the revival of mediaeval styles began about the same time the Romantic Schools were formed in literature. Also, since in literary history, Romanticism is opposed to classicism, it has been convenient to take over the literary nomenclature to designate architecture which is not in the classic tradition.

BIBLIOGRAPHY

Bibliographical Note

There are two main divisions of the bibliography. The first part concerns architecture, and the second literature.

Since modern buildings in mediaeval styles are the basic source material for a study of Gothic Revival architecture, a chronological list of some of the more noted examples precede the bibliography proper. They are listed geographically, namely under the headings, England, France, Germany and the United States, as are the two following sections of the first division.

The first section gives a chronological list of books which aided the architect in his knowledge of mediaeval architecture. They are also basic source material for a study of the Gothic Revival. Next comes an alphabetical list of secondary works on the Gothic Revival. A group of art histories which include the period under consideration concludes the first division. This is annotated throughout.

The first section of the second part of the bibliography lists chronologically a few of the more important literary productions of the Romantic period which had a direct influence upon the vogue for the Middle Ages and hence were helpful in establishing the Gothic Revival. The second section lists alphabetically some of the secondary works on romanticism and the Romantic period which have been used in this work.

I. *Key Examples of Gothic Revival Architecture*

A. ENGLAND

1753–76 Strawberry Hill. Twickenham. Walpole, Bentley & Chute.

1780   Asbury. Sir Roger Newdigate.

1782   Lee Priory. Kent. James Wyatt.
1792   St. Peter's Chapel. Winchester. Milner & Carter.
1795–99 Fonthill Abbey. Wiltshire. Wyatt.
1803   Killy Moon, Co. Tyrone. Ireland. Nash.
1806–13 Ashridge. Hertfordshire. Wyatt.
1811   East Cowes Castle. Isle of Wight. Nash.
1812   Abbotsford. Scotland. Atkinson.
1822   St. George. Birmingham. Rickman.
1824   St. Luke's. Chelsea. Savage.
1826   St. Peter's. Brighton. Barry.
1827–31 New Building, St. John's College. Cambridge. Rickman.
1839–45 Parliament Buildings. London. Barry & Pugin.
1841   St. Chad's. Birmingham. Pugin.
1849–50 All Saints Church, Margaret St. London. Butterfield.
1851   St. Augustine's. Ramsgate. Pugin.
1859   Assize Courts & Town Hall. Manchester. Waterhouse.
1860   The Red House, for Wm. Morris, Bixley Heath. Kent. Philip Webb.
1861   Offices, No. 19, Lincolns Inn Fields. London. Philip Webb.
1864–72 Albert Memorial. London. G. G. Scott.
1868–84 New Law Courts. London. Street.
1874–84 Cathedral. Edinburgh. G. G. Scott.
1880–1910 Truro Cathedral. Truro. Pearson.
1904–   Liverpool Cathedral. Liverpool. Giles G. Scott.

B. FRANCE

1787   Gardens of the Prince de Montbéliard. Alsace. Kléber.
1816–47 Chapelle d'Orleans. Dreux. Percier & Lafranc.
1819   Tomb of Abelard & Héloise. Père Lachaise, Paris. Lenoir.
1821   Decorations for the Baptism of the duc de Bordeaux.
1825   Decorations for the coronation of Charles X at Reims.
1826   Château de la Reine Blanche. Chantilly. Fontaine.
1835   Church of Montmartre. Paris. Comte de l'Escalofier.
1843   St. Ferdinand. Paris. Fontaine.

1846–59 Ste-Clotilde. Paris. Gau & Ballu.
1875–89 Bascilica. Lourdes. Daraud.

C. GERMANY

1818–21 Denkmal auf dem Kreuzberg. Berlin. Schinkel.
1825–30 Werder Kirche. Berlin. Schinkel.
1829–43 Ludwigskirche. Munich. von Gartner.
1831–39 St. Mariahilfkirche. Munich. Ohlmüller.
1838   Schloss Babelsberg. Potsdam. Strack & Persius.
1842–80 New part of Cologne Cathedral. Cologne. Zwirner &
         Voigtel.
1844   Nicolaikirche. Hamburg. G. G. Scott.
1844   Jacobikirche. Berlin. Stüler.
1845–47 Catholic Church. Leipzig. Heideloff.
1846–50 Petrikirche. Berlin. Strack.
1853–79 Votivkirche. Vienna. von Ferstel.
1860   Rathaus. Berlin. Waesemann.
1860   Christ Church. Hanover. Hase.
1860   Postoffice. Hildesheim. Hase & Oppler.
1864–69 St. Thomas Church. Berlin. Adler.
1866   Kreuzschule. Dresden. C. F. Arnold.
1866   Villa Sloman. Hamburg. Jolasse.
1867–68 Villa March. Charlottenburg. Heuse.
1872–83 Rathaus. Vienna. von Schmidt.
1873–83 Parliament Buildings. Budapest. Steindl.
1881   Stiftungshaus. Vienna. von Schmidt.
1885–88 Church of the Holy Cross. Berlin. Otzen.

D. UNITED STATES

1799   Sedgeley, country mansion. Philadelphia. Latrobe.
1807   Chapel, St. Mary's Seminary. Baltimore. Godefroy.
1823–25 Trinity Church. Pittsburgh. Hopkins.
1823   St. Stephens. Philadelphia. Strickland.
1832   Glenn Ellen, country mansion. Baltimore. A. J. Davis.
1833   First Parish Church. Cambridge. Isaiah Rogers.
1833–36 New York University. New York. A. J. Davis.

1836   Rotch House. New Bedford. A. J. Davis.

1839–46 Trinity Church. New York. R. Upjohn.

1842   Gore Hall, Library. Cambridge.

1847   State House. Baton Rouge. Renwick.

1843–46 Grace Church. New York. Renwick.

1848   St. Mark's. Philadelphia. John Notman.

1850–79 St. Patrick's Cathedral. New York. Renwick.

1852   Smithsonian Institute. Washington. Renwick.

1860   Entrance to Greenwood Cemetery. Brooklyn. R. Upjohn.

1865   Central Congregational Church. Boston. R. M. Upjohn.

1870–77 Memorial Hall, Harvard. Cambridge. Wade.

1872   Trinity Church. Boston. Richardson.

1873–78 State House. Hartford. R. M. Upjohn.

1884   Allegheny Court House. Pittsburgh. Richardson.

1891   University of Chicago. Chicago. H. I. Cobb.

1892   All Saints Chapel. Ashmont, Mass. Cram & Goodhue.

1892–   St. John the Divine. New York. LaFarge, since 1927, Cram.

1913–28 Swedenborgian Cathedral. Bryn Athyn, Pa. Cram & Pitcairn.

II. *Primary Sources*

A. ENGLAND

The Gentleman's Magazine, edited by Sylvanus Urban. London, 1731–1907.

The first article which praises the Gothic appeared in December, 1739. From then until 1850, an increasing number of antiquarian and archaeological essays appear. As the printing of illustrations becomes more prevalent, more cuts are devoted to architecture, and most particularly, mediaeval. It seems that this magazine must have played an important role both in spreading the vogue for the mediaeval in the eighteenth century and in encouraging the Gothic Revivalists of the first half of the nineteenth century.

LANGLEY, BATTY AND THOMAS. *Ancient Architecture Restored and Improved.* London, 1742.

LANGLEY, BATTY AND THOMAS. *Gothic Architecture Improved.* 2nd ed. of foregoing work with new title. London, 1747.

This is the first architectural work to be devoted to Gothic architecture since the Renaissance. It has been much criticized but it is a sincere attempt to analyze the styles of mediaeval architecture. His historical theories have all been proved wrong. He thought that the Gothic, or Saxon, as he preferred to name it, style was formed before the Danish invasions. Yet, as a pioneer and example of the mid-eighteenth century fad for the Gothic, it is important.

Some Designs of Mr. Inigo Jones and Mr. Wm. Kent. Published by John Vardy, London, 1744.

Dr. Fiske Kimball lent me his copy of this interesting publication which contains Kent's early Gothic design for the Courts of Chancery and King's Bench on the Dais of Westminster Hall, submitted February 27, 1738/9.

DARLY, M. *A New Book of Chinese, Gothic and Modern Chairs.* London, 1750–51.

HALFPENNY, WILLIAM. *Rural Architecture in the Gothic Taste.* London, 1751.

HALFPENNY, WILLIAM. *Chinese and Gothic Architecture Properly Ornamented.* London, 1752.

CHIPPENDALE, THOMAS. *The Gentleman and Cabinet-Maker's Director.* London, 1754.

DECKER, P. *Gothic Architecture Decorated.* London, 1759.

The five preceding books illustrate the eclectic and adventurous taste of the 1750's. Gothic and Chinese vied with the classical and two or three styles were used together. Architectural ornament was affected, but even more interior decoration and the sham buildings which dotted the picturesque gardens.

WALPOLE, HORACE. *Anecdotes of Painting in England.* Strawberry Hill, 1762–71.

This work was based on the notes of George Vertue, the engraver and antiquary, who for forty years gathered notes for the history of art in England. It is more than antiquarian or archaeological, but also attempts the aesthetic interpretation of art.

BENTHAM, JAMES. *History and Antiquities of the Conventual and Cathedral Church of Ely.* Cambridge, 1771.

An excellent guide and the forerunner of many similar studies.

GROSE, FRANCIS. *Antiquities of England and Wales.* 4 vols. London, 1773–76.

The encyclopedic attitude of mind flourished in the latter eighteenth century. Nowhere is this attitude better exemplified than by Grose, although he is not so well known as Diderot and Johnson. His volumes seem tedious and heavy nowadays, but he must have been influential in preparing the interest in the past which makes such an excellent culture-medium for romanticism.

A Description of the Villa of Mr. Horace Walpole at Strawberry-Hill near Twickenham and Middlesex. With an Inventory of the Furniture, Pictures, Curiosities, Etc. Strawberry Hill, 1774.

This catalogue is a good reason why Walpole's Gothic has overshadowed the Gothicisms of his contemporaries, until today he holds an unduly prominent position in the development of the Gothic Revival.

CARTER, J. *Specimens of the Ancient Sculpture and Painting Now Remaining in this Kingdom.* London, 1780.

An interesting collection of mediaeval art and the first book of "specimens."

GROSE, FRANCIS. *Antiquities of Ireland.* London, 1791.

HALFPENNY, JOSEPH. *Gothic Ornaments in the Cathedral Church of York.* York, 1795.

Good plates.

GROSE, FRANCIS. *Antiquities of Scotland.* London, 1797.

This book was published after Grose's death. Grose, when in Scotland gathering material for this work, inspired Burns to write, "There's a chiel amang you taking notes."

MILNER, JOHN. *History of Winchester.* 2 vols. Winchester, 1798.

This history is the classic work on Winchester and is still of value. The author was a Roman Catholic bishop of Castabala, and firmly felt that Gothic was a Catholic style. He was a Revivalist in that he had the Chapel of St. Peter built in the Gothic style.

BENTHAM and WILLIS. *History of Gothic and Saxon Architecture in England.* London, 1798.

An attempt to discriminate periods.

WARTON, BENTHAM, GROSE and MILNER. *Essays on Gothic Architecture.* London.

A collection of the most famous essays which had appeared on mediaeval architecture in the eighteenth century.

LUGAR, R. *The Country Gentleman's Architect.* London, 1807.
One of the first of the many architectural handbooks for the layman which advocated the picturesque Gothic styles for country villas.

BRITTON, JOHN. *Architectural Antiquities.* 5 vols. London, 1807–26.
Britton is an example of a man who began with nothing, but who by catering to current taste, ended with a fortune derived from his publications. The drawings for his series are good, and it is a pleasure to leaf through the volumes. His publications played an important part in adapting taste to Gothic.

BRITTON, JOHN. *History and Antiquities of the English Cathedral Churches.* 4 vols. London, 1814–35.

RICKMAN, THOMAS. *An Attempt to Discriminate the Styles of English Architecture from the Conquest to the Reformation.* London, 1819.
A most important book, for in it are given the divisions into Norman, Early English, Decorated and Perpendicular of English mediaeval architecture, which classification is still in use.

PUGIN, AUGUSTUS. *Specimens of Gothic Architecture.* Descriptions by E. J. Willson. London, vol. 1, 1821, vol. 2, 1823.
These volumes with the preceding work of Rickman are the reason for dating the Gothic Revival from 1820. They enabled the architects to begin working with archeological correctness. The plates are all geometric drawings done to scale. The architect could now make a mathematically correct copy.

RUTTER, JOHN. *An Illustrated History and Description of Fonthill Abbey.* Shaftsbury, 1823.
Fonthill Abbey vies with Strawberry Hill in the memories of men. It fell down two years after this publication, but this guide and another anonymous one are sufficient to give it partial immortality, especially since there are excellent plates.

ROBINSON, P. F. *Rural Architecture.* London, 1823.
This book was extensively used both in England and North America. The picturesque villas which he illustrates dotted the countryside and numbers of them are still to be seen.

BRITTON, JOHN. *History and Antiquities of Bath Abbey.* London, 1825.

BELL, THOMAS. *An Essay on the Origin and Progress of Gothick Architecture.* Dublin, 1826.
A summary of architectural theory.

Pugin, Augustus. *Gothic Furniture*. London, 1827.
> This book and the younger Pugin's Gothic furniture for Windsor Castle started the nineteenth-century vogue mediaeval furnishings.

Hunt, Thomas F. *Designs for Parsonage Houses*. London, 1827.
> A much used book for with the new churches, new rectories had to be built.

Pugin, Augustus. *Gothic Ornaments*. London, 1831.
> Like all the Pugin books, this was of immediate practical value.

The Architectural Magazine. Conducted by J. C. Loudon. 5 vols. London, 1834–38.
> A great disseminator of Gothic design, extensively used by architects.

Britton, J. *Chronological History and Graphic Illustrations of Christian Architecture in England*. London, 1835.
> Of value to the layman, as an aid in differentiating styles.

Loudon, J. C. *An Encyclopaedia of Cottage Farm and Villa Architecture and Furniture*. London, 1835.
> A compendium for the contractor and furniture manufacturer.

Pugin, A. W. *Gothic Furniture in the Style of the XV Century*. London, 1835.
> The first of the younger Pugin's publication and an immediate success.

Caveler, William. *Select Specimens of Gothic Architecture*. 4 vols. London, 1835–36.
> Some of the select specimens seem rather strange now.

Pugin, A. W. *Contrasts*. London, 1836. 2nd revised edition, London, 1841.
> One of the most brilliant and stimulating books written by an architect, glowing with the fiery zeal and enthusiasm of a convert to Rome. The central theme that the world and art were good before the Reformation and the Renaissance perverted religion and aesthetics has since been often echoed by Catholic historians. The plates contrasting fifteenth and nineteenth-century architecture are as good propaganda as the text.

Pugin, A. W. *Details of Ancient Timber Houses of the XV and XVI Centuries*. London, 1836.

Pugin, A. W. *Designs for Gold and Silversmiths*. London, 1836.

Pugin, A. W. *Designs for Iron and Brass Work in the Style of the XV and XVI Centuries*. London, 1836.
> These books by Pugin had a great influence on design and ornament.

ROBINSON, P. F. *Domestic Architecture in the Tudor Style.* London, 1837.

The Tudor style was always the most popular for private houses.

BRITTON, J. *Dictionary of the Architecture and Archaeology of the Middle Ages.* London, 1838.

This work shows how the attitude toward the Middle Ages was changing from the picturesque to the more scientific study of archaeology.

PUGIN, A. W. *The True Principles of Pointed or Christian Architecture.* London, 1841.

An analysis of the structural elements of mediaeval building which preceded the more famous study of Viollet-le-Duc. Pugin's emphasis on sound construction and organic ornament is sometimes considered the beginning of the contemporary architectural styles of Functionalism and Constructionism.

Ecclesiologist. Vols. 1–3. Cambridge, Nov. 1841–Sept. 1844. New series, vols. 1–26. London, Jan. 1845–Dec. 1868.

The life of this periodical exactly parallels the height of the Gothic Revival. It is the best source of information concerning the ecclesiastical building of the period and clearly defines the aims and aspirations of the movement.

NEALE, JOHN MASON. *A Few Words to Church Builders.* Cambridge, 1841.

The views of the Cambridge Camden Society are here given briefly and succinctly. It aided the introduction of church furniture and church restoration.

MARKLAND, J. H. *Remarks on English Churches.* Oxford, 1843.

This work is really a plea for more suitable and beautiful sepulchral monuments and a heated criticism of contemporary monuments and church furniture in general.

DURANTIS, GULIELMUS, Bp. of Mende, ca 1237–1296. *The Symbolism of Churches and Church Ornaments.* Trans. by J. M. Neale and Benj. Webb. Leeds, 1843.

This translation of one of the earliest books on church symbolism was of great value in supporting the views of the Ecclesiologists.

PUGIN, A. W. *Present State of Ecclesiastical Architecture in England.* London, 1843.

PUGIN, A. W. *An Apology for the Revival of Christian Architecture in England.* London, 1843.

The first book points out in what a bad state architecture is and the second shows how it can be improved by a sincere and conscientious rival of "Christian" styles.

The Builder. An illustrated weekly magazine. Vols. 1–145. London, 1843–1933.
A good source for the changing styles of modern Gothic.

PALEY, F. A. *A Manual of Gothic Architecture.* London, 1846.
A concise guide which went through many editions.

BRANDON, RAPHAEL and J. ARTHUR. *An Analysis of Gothic Architecture.* 2 vols. London, 1847.
Volumes of useful plates.

Instrumenta Ecclesiastica. Edited by the Ecclesiological Society. London, 1847.
A guide explaining church ornament by church liturgy.

RUSKIN, JOHN. *Seven Lamps of Architecture.* London, 1849.
A popular book on architecture which destroyed the last vestiges of style as a criterion and substituted personal and psychological standards.

PUGIN, A. W. *A Treatise on Chancel Screens and Rood Lofts.* London, 1851.
An historical work with excellent plates.

RUSKIN, J. *Stones of Venice.* 2 vols. London, 1851–53.
The most famous chapter in this work is that entitled "The Nature of Gothic." The detailed and enthusiastic account of the development of architecture in Venice aided greatly the vogue for mediaeval Italian styles which characterize so much of the Victorian Gothic.

STREET, G. E. *Brick and Marble in the Middle Ages.* London, 1855.
This study of polychrome facing in the Middle Ages was influential in forming the streaky bacon style which became prevalent in the latter nineteenth century.

COLLING, J. K. *Details of Gothic Architecture.* London, 1856.
A scholarly and careful work which shows the growing eclecticism of Victorian taste which was no longer content with using only English Gothic, but enjoyed continental Gothic as well.

SCOTT, GEORGE GILBERT. *On Gothic Architecture, Secular and Domestic.* London, 1857.
This work was widely read since it was written by the foremost Gothic Revivalist. In large measure, it restates the ideas of A. W. Pugin, but without any controversial bias.

NESFIELD, W. EDEN. *Specimens of Mediaeval Architecture.* London, 1862.
The specimens are continental. The Gothic Revival is no longer a

revival of the old English styles, but has become avowedly eclectic. This is a fitting book with which to end this list for Nesfield and Shaw were responsible for the Queen Anne style which succeeded the Gothic Revival.

B. FRANCE

LENOIR, ALEXANDRE. *Déscription historique et chronologique des Monumens de Sculpture réunis au Musée des Monumens français.* Paris, 1800–06.

The formation of the museum was of even more importance in molding popular taste than the catalogue, which, however, should not be underrated since it went through seven editions by 1803, and is in itself a monument of the learning and enterprise of Lenoir. It is important, also, in that it was one of the first attempts to give a detailed and exact description of mediaeval sculpture.

LABORDE, JOSEPH, COMTE DE. *Les Monumens de la France.* 2 vols. Paris, 1816–36.

A collection of plates and descriptions of the ancient buildings of France, which enabled the untraveled Frenchman to learn what a wealth of architecture there was in his own country.

TAYLOR, ISIDOR JUSTIN SEVERIN, BARON. *Voyages pittoresques et romantiques dans l'ancienne France.* 24 vols. Paris, 1820–63.

A series of volumes similar to the preceding, but which included many more examples. The text is largely by Charles Nodier, a well-known Romantic.

VITET, LUDOVIC. *Rapport à M. le Ministre de l'Interieur sur les Monumens, les Bibliothéques, les archivs et les Musées des Departements de l'Oise, de l'Aisne, de la Marne, du Nord et du Pas-de-Calais.* Paris, 1831.

This report is of interest, since it is the first step which led to the formation of the Commission des Monuments Historiques, which in turn was directly responsible for the widespread restoration of mediaeval buildings in France. It is also worthy of note, since it shows how quickly the politicians of the July Monarchy put into practical effect their interest in the Middle Ages. (Vitet's use of Ludovic, instead of his baptismal name of Louis, indicates how moyenâgeux he was.)

MONTALEMBERT, CHARLES, COMTE DE. *De l'État actuel de l'Art religieux en France.* Paris, 1839.

A book which has two aims: one to criticize the present, the other to praise the past.

MÉRIMÉE, PROSPER. *Études sur les Arts au Moyen Age.* Paris, 1837–61.

Mérimée was the second director of the Commission des Monuments Historiques. It was owing to him the Viollet-le-Duc received his first commission at Vézelay. These studies on mediaeval art were widely read and formed popular ideas until recently when the theories of the archaeologists have become more widespread.

Revue Generale de l'Architecture. Vols. 1–30. Paris, 1840–73.

Interesting as it shows how little the Gothic vogue affected the architect.

VITET, LUDOVIC. *Monographie de l'Église Notre-Dame de Noyon.* Paris, 1845.

VITET, LUDOVIC. *Études sur les Beaux-Arts.* Paris, 1846.

Vitet was the first head of the Commission des Monuments Historiques. His monograph is the forerunner of many others, so that now a special study is obtainable for almost every ancient building in France.

VIOLLET-LE-DUC, E. E. *Dictionnaire raisonné de l'Architecture Français.* 10 vols. Paris, 1854–68.

VIOLLET-LE-DUC, E. E. *Dictionnaire raisonné du Mobilier Français.* 6 vols. Paris, 1858–75.

VIOLLET-LE-DUC, E. E. *Compositions et Dessins.* Paris, 1884.

Viollet-le-Duc was but one of a large group of French architects who devoted most of their time to the restoration of mediaeval buildings. The reason that his name is so much better known than his confreres is that he edited and wrote in large part these dictionaries which are standard works and which are referred to, even if not read, wherever there is a study of mediaeval art.

C. GERMANY

Von Deutscher Art und Kunst, einige fliegende Blätter. Strassburg, 1773.

Herder was responsible for the publication of this anonymous collection of essays, which formulated the principles of the *ältere Romantik* in Germany. Herder wrote three essays, Möser one, Goethe one and one was translated from the Italian of Frisi. Each essay is of great importance in the development of romanticism; and the essay by Goethe on Strassburg Cathedral is of special interest to the Gothic Revivalist.

SCHLEGEL, FRIEDRICH. Aesthetic and Philosophical Writings. Bohm Library, London.

Despite the interest of the old Romantics in the Middle Ages and in

Christianity, and in early German painting, there was very little written about architecture, therefore these notes by Schlegel are of special importance.

BOISSERÉE, SULPIZ. *Histoire et Déscription de la Cathédrale de Cologne, accompagnée de Récherches sur l'Architecture des anciennes Cathédrales.* Stuttgart and Paris, 1823.
Diagrams and Atlas of XVIII plates. Stuttgart, 1821.
This publication of plates and text was more responsible for modern Gothic in Germany than any other one factor. The enthusiasm and interest caused by this work lead to the beginning of the restoration and completion of the cathedral. The group of architects who worked on the cathedral received their apprenticeship in the Gothic there and so by the middle of the century were able to begin designing modern mediaeval.

D. UNITED STATES

HOPKINS, JOHN HENRY. *Essay on Gothic Architecture.* Burlington, Vt., 1836.
The first essay on the Gothic which appeared in the United States, written by an Episcopal clergyman who was an ardent Gothic Revivalist.

DOWNING, A. J. *A Treatise on the Theory of Landscape Gardening.* New York, 1841.
Downing later became editor of the periodical, *The Horticulturalist.* He did a great deal to promote an interest in gardening. His taste ran to the picturesque. In the following book, he advocates the use of the Gothic for the country villa.

DOWNING, A. J. *Cottage Residences.* New York, 1842.

OWEN, ROBERT DALE. *Hints on Public Architecture.* New York, 1849.
Owen was secretary of the building committee of the Smithsonian Institution. The purpose of this book is to prove that the mediaeval styles are cheaper and more practical for modern buildings than the classical.

ARNOT, D. H. *Gothic Architecture Applied to Modern Residences.* New York, 1851.
A persuasive plea for Gothic with drawings by the author.

UPJOHN, RICHARD. *Upjohn's Rural Architecture.* New York, 1852.
Upjohn was a popular architect who transplanted many of the ideas of the English Revivalists to this country.

CRAM, RALPH ADAM. *Church Building*. Boston, 1901.
The foremost contemporary mediaevalist and exponent of original Gothic. He has been influenced both by the English school and the French archaeologists.

ADAMS, HENRY. *Mont Saint Michel and Chartres*. Boston, 1905.
This book, although not primarily architectural, has had great influence in inclining Americans toward the Middle Ages and in keeping alive the taste for modern Gothic.

CRAM, RALPH ADAMS. *The Gothic Quest*. New York, 1907.

CRAM, RALPH ADAMS. *The Substance of Gothic*. Boston, 1917.
Two books which give a most enthusiastic interpretation of Gothic and which have had an important influence in continuing the use of mediaeval styles for churches and scholastic buildings.

III. *Secondary Works on the Gothic Revival*

A. ENGLAND

ALLEN, B. SPRAGUE. *Tides in English Taste, 1619–1800*. 2 vols. Cambridge, 1937.
Volume two gives an excellent account of the pre-Walpole interest in Gothic and the Middle Ages.

An Eighteenth Century Correspondence. Edited by Lillian Dickins and Mary Stanton. London, 1910.
A collection of letters to Sanderson Miller, an amateur of the mediaeval and designer of houses and sham ruins in the Gothic style from 1744 to 1760.

AYSCOUGH, SAMUEL. *General Index to 56 Volumes of the Gentleman's Magazine. 1731–1786*. 2 vols. London, 1818.
Since the *Gentleman's Magazine* is such an important source for a study of the Gothic Revival, this complete and thorough index is of great value.

BETJEMAN, JOHN. *Ghastly Good Taste or, A depressing story of the Rise and Fall of English Architecture*. London, 1933.
A survey of nineteenth-century architecture by an architectural critic, who does not enjoy the subject and who makes incorrect statements.

BLOMFIELD, REGINALD. *Renaissance Architecture in England, 1500–1800*. London, 1900.
Gives the best account of seventeenth-century English Gothic, chap. 7.

BRITTON, JOHN. *Auto-Biography.* 2 vols. London, 1849–50.
The life of the noted publisher of architectural plates, throws sidelights on the early phases of the Gothic Revival.

CESCINSKY, HERBERT. *English Furniture of the Eighteenth Century.* Vol. 2. London, n.d.
Chapter XII, p. 244, discusses Chippendale Gothic and fretted furniture.

CLARK, KENNETH. *The Gothic Revival.* New York, 1929.
A very brilliant book which gives the history of the change in taste in England from 1720 to 1870. The second book written on the subject. Well illustrated.

DALE, ANTHONY. *James Wyatt, Architect, 1746–1813.* Oxford, 1936.
The first full length biography of Wyatt. The author presents impartially the story of his restorations and Gothicisms.

Dictionary of National Biography. Edited by Sidney Lee. New York, 1885–1900.
Articles on Charles Barry, James Essex, Batty Langley, George Vertue, James Wyatt and Sir Jeffrey Wyatville, etc.

EASTLAKE, CHARLES L. *A History of the Gothic Revival.* London, 1872.
The first and only book giving a detailed history of the Gothic Revival in England. Absolutely indispensable.

FERREY, B. *Recollections of A. N. Welby Pugin and of His Father Augustus Pugin.* London, 1861.
Source of most of our information concerning A. W. Pugin, written by a fellow student in his father's school.

The Ford Times. Vol. 13, No. 5, May, 1936.
On page 268, there is an article on St. Augustine's Abbey, Ramsgate, which praises highly this monument of the Gothic Revival and Pugin.

GODFREY, WALTER H. *The Story of Architecture in England.* New York, 1928.
Gives a brief account of the Gothic Revival.

GOODHART–RENDEL, H. S. "English Gothic Architecture of the Nineteenth Century" in the *Journal of the Royal Institute of British Architects.* XXXI: 2, pp. 321–339. April, 1924.
The first twentieth-century defense of nineteenth-century Gothic.

HOPE, SIR WM. HENRY ST. JOHN. *Windsor Castle.* 2 vols. and portfolio of VIII plans. London, 113.
The definitive work on Windsor Castle; especially interesting for the detailed description of nineteenth-century restorations and additions.

HUSSEY, CHRISTOPHER. *The Picturesque.* London and New York, 1927.
A history of eighteenth-century taste which gives an excellent account of the early Gothic vogue and the background of the later Gothic Revival.

KIMBALL, FISKE. "Wm. Kent's Designs for the Houses of Parliament, 1734–40." *Journal of the Royal Institute of British Architects.* Sept. 1932.

KIMBALL, FISKE AND DONNELL, EDNA. "Creators of the Chippendale Style." *Metropolitan Museum Studies,* I:115–154, II:41–59.
Articles about the Gothic furniture designed before Chippendale.

LETHABY, W. R. *Philip Webb and His Work.* London, 1935.
This, the last work of the dean of English architectural historians, includes brief summaries of the work of the leading Gothic Revivalists, as well as giving a most sympathetic account of Webb, who most faithfully tried to follow the principle of sound building, and is therefore more highly considered at present than most of his contemporaries.

LEWIS, W. S. "Genesis of Strawberry Hill." *Metropolitan Museum Studies.* Vol. 5, pt. 1, pp. 57–92, June 1934.
Most interesting article on the designs and plans of Strawberry Hill, greatly enhanced by reproductions of the original Bentley drawings which are now in the possession of Mr. Lewis of Farmington, Conn.

MANWARING, ELIZABETH WHEELER. *Italian Landscape in Eighteenth Century England.* New York, 1925.

MUTHESIUS, HERMAN. *Die neuere kirchliche Baukunst in England.* Berlin, 1901.
A good work, based largely on Eastlake with more stylistic analysis.

NICHOLS, JOHN. *General Index of the Gentleman's Magazine, 1787–1818.* 2 vols. London, 1821.
Thirty-one articles on Gothic architecture to fourteen on Grecian, which gives a good indication of the mediaeval bias of the magazine and why it is of such interest to the student of the Gothic Revival.

Parentalia; or Memoirs of the Family of the Wrens. Published by Stephen Wren. London, 1750.

PLAISTED, ARTHUR H. *English Architecture in a Country Village.* London, 1927.
A chronological study of the best buildings in Medmenham, including the Gothic Revival edifices, one of which was designed by Pugin.

PUGIN, E. W. *Who Was the Art Architect of the Houses of Parliament?* London, 1867.
This unnecessary pamphlet by A. W. Pugin's son caused a great flurry, for it accused Barry of getting all the credit, while Pugin did all the work, neither of which statements was correct.

ROPE, HENRY, E. G. *Pugin.* St. Dominic's Press, Ditchling, Hassocks, Sussex, 1935.
A Catholic eulogy of a Catholic convert.

SCOTT, GEOFFREY. *The Architecture of Humanism.* Boston. 1914.
Scott is a humanist and ardent admirer of Renaissance architecture. He heartly disapproved of the influence of Romantic criticism on architecture and gives a most penetrating analysis of the architectural fallacies of the nineteenth century.

SCOTT, GEORGE GILBERT. *Personal and Professional Recollections.* Edited by G. Gilbert Scott. London, 1879.
Important as it gives the life of the most prolific architect of the Gothic Revival.

SIRR, HARRY. *Augustus Welby Pugin: a Sketch.* London, 1918.
Brief but accurate account of Pugin's life and work.

STEEGMAN, JOHN. *The Rule of Taste from George I to George IV.* London, 1936.
A delightful book on the vagaries of taste in the eighteenth century.

SUMMERSON, JOHN. *John Nash, Architect to King George IV.* London, 1935.
An excellent biography which treats briefly but well Nash's experiments with the Gothic and his relations to the elder Pugin.

TALLMADGE, THOMAS E. *The Story of England's Architecture.* London, 1935.
The author recognizes that both the Greek and Gothic revivals were both expressions of romanticism, and gives a good, brief account of them.

TRAPPES-LOMAX, MICHAEL. *Pugin, The Portrait of a Mediaeval Victorian.* London, 1933.
This is a very useful study of Pugin, since the author gives a list of the buildings which he designed and a bibliography of his writings.

WATERHOUSE, PAUL. "Pugin." *Architectural Review.* Articles in vols. 3 and 4, 1898.
One of the early appreciations of Pugin's work, especially of his ideal of sound construction.

WINGFIELD-STRAFORD, ESME. *Those Earnest Victorians.* New York, 1930.
Chapter XIX, pp. 227–241, entitled "The Gothic Revival," gives an inaccurate, superficial and prejudiced account of the movement.

YVON, PAUL. *La Vie d'un Dilettante: Horace Walpole.* Caen, 1924.
A charming and scholarly study of Walpole with a good account of his Gothicizing propensities.

B. FRANCE

ABRAHAM, POL. *Viollet-le-Duc et le Rationalism mediéval.* Paris, 1934.
A criticism of Violle-le-Duc's theory of Gothic vaulting and mediaeval construction.

ANTHYME, ST-PAUL. *Viollet-le-Duc.* Paris, 1881.
Biography.

Description de l'Église Ste-Clotilde. Paris, 1857.
Pamphlet published soon after the completion of the church and giving best detailed account of it.

GOUT, PAUL ÉMILE. *Viollet-le-Duc.* Paris, 1914.
Appreciation and biography.

HAUTECOUER, AUBERT et REY. *Le Romantisme et l'Art.* Paris, 1928.
The part by Marcel Aubert on the mediaevalism of the Romantic period gives the best general account that I have found.

LANSON, RENÉ. *Le Goût du Moyen Age en France au XVIIIe Siècle.* Paris, 1926.
Best, most informative book on the subject.

MAIGRON, LOUIS. *Le Romantisme et la Mode.* Paris, 1911.
An excellent study based on contemporary documents of the vagaries of fashion and the mediaeval fad of the period about 1830.

REYBAUD, LOUIS. *Jérôme Paturot à la Récherche d'une Position sociale.* Paris, 1843.
Delicious satire of the many phases of romanticism. The chapters which tell of Paturot's attempt to have a Gothic house are of special interest.

ROBIQUET, JACQUES. *L'Art et le Goût sous la Restauration 1814–1830.* Paris, 1928.
A well documented but not particularly illuminating study.

ROSENTHAL, LEON. *L'Art et les Artistes Romantiques.* Paris, 1928.

Deals mostly with painters.

SCHOMMER, P. *L'Art decoratif du Temps du Romantisme.* Brussels, 1928.

Very good study of decorative fashions.

C. GERMANY

BAUR, WILHELM. *Geschichts- und Lebensbilder.* 5th ed. 2 vols. in one, Hamburg, 1893.

Vol. 2, chapter 12, pp. 331–354 gives the biography of Sulpiz Boisserée.

JOSEPH, DAVID. *Geschichte der Baukunst von Altertum bis zur Neuzeit.* Vol. 4. Berlin, 1912.

Joseph gives the fullest account of modern Gothic in Germany that is to be found.

NARJOUX, FELIX. *A Journey of an Architect in the Northwest of Europe.* Trans. by John Peto. Boston, 1877.

Narjoux was an eminent French architect; student of and later collaborator with Viollet-le-Duc. In 1874, he made a trip through northern Germany to study their buildings of modern Gothic and to make sketches, 214 of which are reproduced.

D. UNITED STATES

COOK, CLARENCE. "Architecture in America," *The North American Review.* No. 310, September, 1882.

The author finds the current fad for French Renaissance just as ridiculous as the previous vogues for Roman, Egyptian and Gothic.

COOLIDGE, JOHN, JR. *Gothic Revival Churches in the United States, 1823–1892.* Thesis in MS in Library of Harvard Architectural School, Cambridge, Mass.

Following the idea of his professor, Leonard Updycke, Coolidge considers the Gothic Revival to be the last stage of Renaissance art. He has photographed and gathered information about a goodly number of nineteenth-century churches. A very good study, which I hope will be published.

CRAM, RALPH ADAMS. *My Life in Architecture.* Boston, 1936.

Most interesting autobiography as it gives the personal account of the foremost Gothic Revivalist of the present.

DONNELL, EDNA. "A. J. Davis and the Gothic Revival." *Metropolitan Museum Studies.* Vol. 5, pt. 2, pp. 183–233, Sept. 1936.
So far as I know this is the first study of a lesser known American architect of the middle nineteenth-century who worked almost exclusively in mediaeval styles.

EDGELL, G. H. *The American Architecture of To-day.* New York, 1928.
Has a few scathing remarks on American Gothic.

HAMLIN, TALBOT, F. *The American Spirit in Architecture.* New Haven, 1926.
A few paragraphs devoted to the Gothic.

HITCHCOCK, HENRY-RUSSELL, JR. *The Architecture of H. H. Richardson and His Times, 1838–1886.* New York, 1936.
Richardson was the leader of the Romanesque revival in this country. This study is detailed and well illustrated with 145 plates.

KIMBALL, FISKE. *American Architecture.* New York, 1928.
Mr. Kimball is an authority on colonial architecture, yet he has been more interested by the Gothic Revival than most. In this book, chapter IX deals with "Romanticism and the Gothic," a very brief survey of some of the most known examples of American Gothic.

MUMFORD, LEWIS. *The Brown Decades.* New York, 1931.

MUMFORD, LEWIS. *Sticks and Stones.* New York, 1924.
Although neither book deals specifically with American Gothic they both throw many sidelights on American taste and building.

PENTY, A. J. "Authority and Liberty in Architecture." *Journal of the American Institute of Architects.* Vol. 14, pp. 379–383, Sept. 1926.
Discussion of new styles versus traditional with special reference to the Gothic.

RUSH, W. S. "Godefroy and St. Mary's Chapel, Baltimore." *Liturgical Arts.* Vol. 2, 3rd quarter, pp. 140–145.
Brief account of one of the first Gothic Revival buildings in the United States.

STALLWORTH, N. G. *The Development of Secular Gothic Architecture in the United States.* M. A. thesis in Fine Arts, Chicago, 1925.
Discusses chiefly collegiate architecture—well illustrated.

TALLMADGE, THOMAS E. *The Story of Architecture in America.*
New York, 1927.
Brief mention of the Gothic Revival.

Thomas Jefferson, Architect. Original designs in the collection
of Thomas Jefferson Coolidge, Jr., with an essay and notes
by Fiske Kimball. Privately printed, Boston, 1916.
Source for Jefferson's few dabblings with the Gothic.

TURNER, A. A. *Villas on the Hudson.* New York, 1860.
Book of illustrations which show how the picturesque and mediaeval
had invaded the country villa of the mid-nineteenth century.

VAN RENSSELAER, (MRS.) M. G. *Henry Hobson Richardson
and His Works.* Boston, 1888.
First and standard work on Richardson.

WESTCOTT, THOMPSON. *The Historic Mansions and Buildings
of Philadelphia.* Philadelphia, 1877.
Gives an account of Sedgeley, which according to Kimball is the
earliest Gothic Revival building in America.

E. GENERAL HISTORIES WHICH DEAL WITH
THIS PERIOD

BRAULT, ÉLIE. *Les Architectes par leurs Œuvres.* Vol. 3. Paris
[1894].
Volume three gives notices of a large number of little known architects
of the nineteenth-century, as well as of the famous ones.

FAURE, ÉLIE. *History of Art.* Trans. by Walter Pach. Vol. 4
"Modern Art." New York, 1924.
Deals mostly with romanticism in painting in chapters devoted to
early nineteenth-century.

FERGUESSON. *Modern Styles of Architecture.* Edited by Robert
Kerr. 3rd ed. London, 1891.
Ferguesson was a thoroughgoing classicist and had no sympathy for
the uncouth Goth.

FLETCHER, BANNISTER. *A History of Architecture on the Com-
parative Method.* 10th ed. London, 1938.
Gives an excellent brief summary of the Gothic Revival.

HILDEBRANDT, HANS. *Die Kunst des. 19. und 20. Jahrhunderts.*
Wildpark, Potsdam, 1924.
Inexact in the brief account given.

HITCHCOCK, HENRY RUSSELL. *Modern Architecture, Romanticism and Reintegration.* New York, 1929.
Best general account of modern Gothic in England and on the continent.

KIMBALL AND EDGELL. *A History of Architecture.* New York, 1918.
Paragraphs in chapters 12 and 13 deal with modern Gothic in Europe and the United States. The authors use the term Romanticism instead of Gothic Revival.

MICHEL, ANDRÉ. Ed. *Histoire de l'Art.* Vol. 8, 3 pts. Paris, 1925.
Brief accounts of modern Gothic, with most space devoted to France.

PAULI, GUSTAV. *Die Kunst des Klassizismus und der Romantik.* Berlin, 1925.
Good illustrations, text of little value, very few dates.

STURGIS AND FROTHINGHAM. *History of Architecture.* Vol. 4, New York, 1915.
Disregards "neo-gothic," save for a contemptuous sentence on page 325.

SHARP, WILLIAM. *Progress of Art in the Century.* Toronto and Philadelphia, 1906.
Surprising number of inaccuracies in page devoted to Gothic.

UNIVERSITY PRINTS. Series G. M. Modern Architecture. Edited by Kenneth Conant. 1930.
Useful illustrations.

VENTURI, LIONELLO. *History of Art Criticism.* New York, 1936.
Chapter VII, pp. 163–190, "Romanticism and the Middle Ages." He considers Ruskin the culminating point in romantic art criticism.

IV. *Chronological List of Works Which Aided the Gothic Period*

A. ENGLAND

1754	*Essay on Norman Architecture.* Gray.
1761	*The Fatal Sister, the Descent of Odin.* Gray.
1762	*Letters on Chivalry and Romance.* Hurd.
1764	*Castle of Otranto.* Walpole.
1765	*Reliques of Ancient English Poetry.* Percy.
1765	*Poems of Ossian.* MacPherson.

1770   *Poems.* Chatterton.
1794   *Essay on the Picturesque.* Price.
1802   *Minstrelsy of the Scottish Border.* Scott.
1805   *The Lay of the Last Minstrel.* Scott.
1808   *Marmion.* Scott.
1809   *The Lady of the Lake.* Scott.
1809   *Scottish Chiefs.* Porter.
1813   *The Border Antiquities of England and Scotland.* Scott.
1814–32 *Waverley Novels.* Scott.
1843   *Past and Present.* Carlyle.

B. FRANCE

1802   *Le Génie du Christianisme.* Chateaubriand.
1813   *De l'Allemagne.* Madame de Staël.
1812–22 *Histoire des Croisades.* Michaud.
1827   *Lettres sur l'Histoire de France.* Thierry.
1831   *Notre Dame de Paris.* Hugo.
1833–46 *Histoire de France jusqu'au XVI Siècle.* Michelet.
1837–61 *Études sur les Arts au Moyen Age.* Mérimée.

V. *Secondary Works on Romanticism and the Romantic Period*

ABERCROMBIE, LASCELLES. *Romanticism.* New York, 1927.

BABBITT, IRVING. *Rousseau and Romanticism.* Boston, 1919.
   Excellent bibliography.

BAGEHOT, WALTER. *Literary Studies.* Vol. 2. Everyman Library "Wordsworth, Tennyson and Browning; or, Pure, Ornate, and Grotesque Art in English Poetry (1864)" p. 305.

BAUDELAIRE, CHARLES. *L'Art Romantique.* Paris, 1874.

BECHER, CARL L. *The Heavenly City of Eighteenth-Century Philosophers.* New Haven, 1932.

BEERS, HENRY A. *A History of English Romanticism in the Eighteenth Century.* New York, 1899.

BEERS, HENRY A. *A History of English Romanticism in the Nineteenth Century.* New York, 1901.

BIRKHEAD, EDITH. *The Tale of Terror; a Study of Gothic Romance.* New York, 1920.

BRANDES, GEORG. *Wolfgang Goethe.* Trans. by A. W. Porter-field. New York, 1936.

BRINTON, CRANE. *Political Ideas of the English Romanticists.* Oxford, 1926.

BRUNETIERE, F. *Manual of the History of French Literature.* Trans. by Ralph Derechef. New York, 1898.

BRUNOT, MORNOT et HAZARD. *Le Romantisme et les Lettres.* Paris, 1929.

BUTLER, JAMES, R. M. *A History of England 1815–1918.* London, 1928.

COLLINGWOOD, WILLIAM G. *The Life and Work of John Ruskin.* 2 vols. Boston, 1893.

Correspondence of Thomas Gray. Ed. by Toynbee and Whibley. Vol. 1. Oxford, 1935.

CREIGHTON, JAMES E. "Romanticism" in *The Encyclopedia Americana.* New York, 1936.

CROCE, BENEDETTO. *Theory and History of Historiography.* Trans. by Douglas Ainslie. London, 1921.

EASTLAKE, CHARLES L. *Hints on Household Taste.* First American edition. Boston, 1872.
  Fascinating book for it shows to what an eclectic confusion the roman-tic love of change and variety had brought house furnishings and also because it exerted such influence in this country as well as England and prepared the way for Morris and Mission.

FAIRCHILD, H. N. *The Noble Savage.* New York, 1926.

FAIRCHILD, H. N. *The Romantic Quest.* New York, 1931.

GAUTIER, THEOPHILE. *Histoire du Romantisme.* Paris, 1868.

GILL, ERIC. *Art Nonsense and Other Essays.* London, 1929.

GRIERSON, H. J. C. *Classical and Romantic.* Cambridge, 1923.

GUERARD, ALBERT. *French Civilization in the Nineteenth Century.* New York, 1914.

GRUNWALD, CONSTANTIN DE. *Baron Stein, Enemy of Napoleon.* Trans. by C. F. Atkinson. London, 1936.

HAFERKORN, REINHARD. *Gotik und Ruine in der englischen Dichtung des achtzehnten Jahrhunderts.* Leipzig, 1924.

HEINE, HEINRICH. *Germany.* Trans. by C. G. Leland. 2 vols. London, 1892.

The Journal of the Rev. John Wesley A.M. 4 vols. Everyman Library.

JOUSSAIN, ANDRÉ. *Romantisme et Politique.* Paris, 1924.

KRAKOWSKI, EDOUARD. *Les Sources Mediévales de la Philosophie de Locke.* Paris, 1915.

LADD, HENRY ANDREWS. *The Victorian Morality of Art: an Analysis of Ruskin's Esthetic.* New York, 1932.

LAMARTINE, ALPHONSE DE. *Premières Meditations.* Hachette, Paris, 1924.

Of special interest is the preface of July 2, 1849 which gives the history of the formation of the mind of a leading Romanticist.

LAMARTINE, ALPHONSE DE. *Nouvelles Meditations.* Hachette, Paris, 1924.

Again, it is the preface, "A un ami: Dargaul," written in 1840, which is of great value as it shows how a Romanticist thinks.

LUCAS, F. L. *The Decline and Fall of the Romantic Ideal.* New York, 1936.

MAAR, HARKO G. DE. *A History of Modern English Romanticism.* Vol. 1. London, 1924.

Maclise Portrait Gallery, with memoirs by Wm. Bates. London, 1898.

MAIGRON, LOUISE. *Le Roman Historique à l'Epoque Romantique:* essai sur l'influence de Walter Scott. Paris, 1898.

MANNHEIM, KARL. *Ideology and Utopia.* London, 1936.

MARITAIN, JACQUES. *Three Reformers.* New York, 1934.

MOODY AND LOVETT. *A History of English Literature.* New York, 1918.

MORE, P. E. *Drift of Romanticism.* Boston.

MORNET, D. *Le Romantisme en France au 18e siècle.* Paris, 1912.

MOWAT, R. B. *The Romantic Age: Europe in the Early 19th Century.* London, 1937.

NORTHRUP, C. S. "Addison and Gray as Travellers" in *Studies in Language and Literature in Celebration of the Seventieth Birthday of James Morgan Hart*. Pp. 370–439. New York, 1910.

NUEMEYER, ALFRED. "Is there a Romantic Style?" *Parnassus* IX:7, Dec. 1937.

OVERTON, JOHN H. and RELTON, FREDERICK. *The English Church from the Accession of George I to the End of the XVIII Century*. London, 1906.

PERRY, BLISS. *Thomas Carlyle*. Indianapolis, 1915.

PINEYRO AND PEERS. *The Romantics of Spain*. Liverpool, 1934.

RALEIGH, SIR WALTER. *Romance*. Princeton, 1916.

RANDALL, HENRY S. *The Life of Thomas Jefferson*. 3 vols. Philadelphia, 1857.

RASIN, SISTER MARY EUNICE. *Evidences of Romanticism in the Poetry of Mediaeval England*. Doc. thesis. Louisville, Ky., 1929.

REYNAUD, LOUIS. *Le Romantisme*. Paris, 1926.

ROBERTSON, J. G. *The Genesis of Romantic Theory*. Cambridge, 1923.

ROE, FREDERICK W. *The Social Philosophy of Carlyle and Ruskin*. New York, 1921.

SEILLIERE, ERNEST. *Le Mal romantique*. Paris, 1908.

SEILLIERE, ERNEST. *Le Romantisme*. Paris, 1925.

SMITH, LOGAN PEARSALL. *S. P. E. Tract, No. 17*. "Four Words: Romantic, Originality, Creative, Genius." Oxford, 1924.

SMITH, WARREN H. *Architecture in English Fiction*. New Haven, 1934.

SPENGLER, OSWALD. *The Decline of the West*. Trans. by C. F. Atkinson. Vol. 2. New York, 1928.

STRATHERS, MADISON. *Chateaubriand et l'Amerique*. Grenoble, 1905.

STRACHEY, LYTTON. *Queen Victoria*. New York, 1921.

STEPHEN, LESLIE. *History of English Thought in the Eighteenth Century*. 2 vols. London, 1876.

SYKES, NORMAN. *Church and State in England in the XVIII Century.* Cambridge, 1934.

TAINE, H. A. *L'Ancien Régime.* Paris, 1876.

TAINE, H. A. *History of English Literature.* Trans. by N. Van Laun. Vol. 2. Chicago, n.d.

TREITSCHKE, HEINRICH VON. *History of Germany in the Nineteenth Century.* Trans. by Eden and Cedar Paul. Vols. 1 and 2. New York, 1915, 16.

VAN TIEGHEM, PAUL. *Le Movement Romantique.* Paris, 1923.

VOLTAIRE, MR. DE. *Letters Concerning the English Nation.* London, 1731.
French edition. Paris, 1734.

VUY, JULES. *Origine des Idées politique de Rousseau.* 2nd ed. Geneva, 1889.

WHITNEY, LOIS. *Primitivism and the Idea of Progress in English Popular Literature of the eighteenth century.* Baltimore, 1934.

WILENSKI, R. H. *John Ruskin.* London, 1933.

WILLOUGHBY, L. A. *The Romantic Movement in Germany.* Oxford, 1930.

WORDSWORTH, CHRISTOPHER. *Memoirs of William Wordsworth.* 2 vols. London, 1851.

WYNDHAM, GEORGE. *Esays in Romantic Literature.* London, 1919.

INDEX